NUTRITION FOR LIFE

Guide to Gaining Personal Wealth

With Suggestions on Getting Rich, Leadership Skills, and Reaching Goals

by Larry Waschka, Andrew J. DuBrin, and Jeff Davidson

A Division of Macmillan General Reference
A Pearson Education Macmillan Company
1633 Broadway, New York, NY 10019

 For information, address Alpha Books, 1633 Broadway, 7th Floor, New York, NY 10019-6785.

International Standard Book Number: 0-02863703-8

Library of Congress Catalog Card Number is available upon request from the publisher

02 01 00 99 4 3 2 1

Interpretation of the printing code: the rightmost number of the first series of numbers is the year of the book's printing; the rightmost number of the second series of numbers is the number of the book's printing. For example, a printing code of 99-1 shows that the first printing occurred in 1999.

Text is excerpted from *The Complete Idiot's Guide to Getting Rich* (ISBN 0-02-862952-3), *The Complete Idiot's Guide to Leadership* (ISBN 0-02-861946-3), and *The Complete Idiot's Guide to Reaching Your Goals* (ISBN 0-02-862114-X).

Printed in the *United States of America*

Contents

The Basics of Getting Rich

by Larry Waschka

Wouldn't it be nice to win a million-dollar lottery? Just the thought of it might seem nice, but if you really examine how a lottery is paid, you'll probably be surprised. Lottery winners think that they're going to get all the money at one time. Not true. If you win a million-dollar lottery, in most states your payout will be sent to you in yearly increments, minus federal and state taxes, based on your life expectancy. Once you really examine the truth about winning the lottery, you'll find that it's not all that attractive anymore.

The opposite is true with building wealth. I have found that once you really examine the truth about building wealth, it's not only more attractive, it's also a lot easier to achieve than you might think. All you have to do is read and implement the steps, habits, and characteristics needed, and you will be on your way to building wealth.

Introduction

Until I was 25 years old, my dream of getting rich led me to believe that wealth was something you could achieve quickly. Like most people in their teens and twenties, I looked for the lottery win or the windfall that I believed was out there. This illusion becomes reality for only an exclusive handful of people who do actually win the lottery or inherit big sums of money. By the way, if you want to learn how to achieve either of these two dreams, this is not the book for you.

The book you're holding in your hand is not about getting rich fast. It's about gradually building wealth that, if cared for properly, can last for years and even generations to come.

Over the past 13 years, I've spent countless hours studying wealthy people—and not so wealthy people. What I've learned is that the difference has more to do with decisions and habits than it does talent, skill, and intelligence. I know multi-millionaires who never went to college, and I know multi-talented, highly intelligent people who will never become millionaires.

The decision to build wealth is easy to make but may be difficult at times to maintain. It doesn't take a brilliant idea, but it often takes the ability to change your habits and ways of thinking. Old habits are hard to break, and I've seen many times how bad habits ruin a person's chances of ever building significant wealth. The journey takes some effort, and for whatever reason, many people are just not willing to put out the effort necessary to make the change.

What exactly is a strong enough power to change a person's habit? The answer is decision and passion. The decision to build wealth must be accompanied by and aligned with your passion. The first part is easy to do, but the second takes some people a lifetime. You must know your passions. What do you enjoy the most? What excites you? What makes you smile? What would you be willing to do for free? These are the types of questions you must ask yourself. Within the answers you should find several items that will motivate you enough to build the wealth you've always dreamed of. This book will help you find your own passion and motivation.

You can build significant financial wealth with the lessons in this material. I've seen thousands of people do it. However, be sure to focus on the other facets of life just as much. True wealth involves a balanced life. It's a journey, not a destination.

Chapter 1

Are You Going to Be Rich?

In This Chapter

- You're never too old to start
- Real-life rags-to-riches stories
- Do you need a college degree to get rich?
- How adversity can build wealth
- Test your chances of building wealth
- Common misconceptions about wealth

Who would you say is the wealthiest person you know personally? How did he or she achieve the wealth? Is it possible for you to achieve similar wealth? It's as possible as you think it is. Most of the wealthy people I know built their fortunes with their own hands. This is self-made wealth: It's not inherited, acquired through marriage, or won in the lottery. It's built with hard work, determination, and passion.

Self-made wealth is often invisible. You don't see it or recognize it because it's owned by people who don't flaunt it or talk about it. You can learn a lot from these people, but they aren't often featured in magazines or television. They may live next door to you and have an incredible knowledge about building wealth, but you'd never know to ask.

This chapter is about these people. Although I discuss a few wealthy people featured in magazines, most of this chapter is focused on the invisible wealthy people. I dedicate this material to them because they taught me the secrets of building wealth. This chapter will also enable you to find out whether you have what it takes to be wealthy.

Lives of the Rich and Affluent

Most dictionaries define rich as "having an abundance of money." The Commerce Department uses the term *affluent* instead of rich. According to it, if you make more than $75,000 per year, you are considered affluent. Every year, you can find numerous magazine articles featuring people who have achieved affluence.

Time Magazine (2/19/96, p. 42) featured five guys who really scored big in the technology industry. Software designer Marc Andreessen at the age of 24 was worth an estimated $131 million after his company Netscape went public. Netscape's Internet browser called the Navigator was a huge success.

At age 40, Steve Jobs was worth an estimated $728 million after his company Pixar Animation Studios went public. The other three men were worth $22, $79, and $86 million, and all were under the age of 45.

A story in *Cosmopolitan* (5/96, p. 214) featured eight women who became millionaires before the age of 30. Each one did it in a unique way in eight different industries—parking garages, clothing, marketing, stock trading, asbestos abatement, frozen yogurt, computers, and medical screening.

Thirty-four year-old Lisa Renshaw of Baltimore controls 51 parking garages in Maryland, Washington, D.C., and Virginia with $25 million in revenues. She started at 21 years old by renting a parking garage and leasing out spaces herself.

Words of the Wealthy

Wealth is defined by *Webster's Dictionary* as an "abundance of valuable material possessions or resources," and the word wealthy is defined as "extremely affluent." The definition of **affluent** sounds even better, "having a generously sufficient and typically increasing supply of material possessions."

While in Italy studying printmaking and fashion, Jennifer Barclay missed the beginning of her college semester and decided to start a business tie-dying and block-printing cotton clothing and scarves. She went from her parents' garage to a company with $10 million in sales before she turned 29.

Former nurse and aerobics instructor, Karen Behnke, became a millionaire before her 30th birthday by starting a company called Execu-Fit. Her company offered medical screenings of executives and analyses of employee health. She built sales by calling on personnel departments and signing large companies such as Pacific Gas & Electric. When bank loans were impossible, she used credit cards at 22 percent interest. Later, she traded 10 percent of her company for additional capital. In 1993, Karen sold her company to PacifiCare HMO for nearly $5 million.

The *Cosmopolitan* article has more examples such as these. Wealthy people all started their own businesses. However, you don't have to start your own business to be wealthy. Plenty of wealthy people never had their own companies. Sure, starting your own business definitely increases your chances, but it's not a requirement.

Do You Identify with Wealthy People?

Most people can't identify with extremely wealthy people. Either the story is too complicated or it just seems too overwhelming. However, most people can easily identify with real people who built fortunes out of almost nothing. I'm talking about wealthy people who earned every dime they made. Most of them don't wear flashy clothes or drive fancy cars. They don't live in mansions or travel to Paris for a vacation. They live next door to you, and you may not even know their names. Most of my clients fit this description. Some of these people drive old trucks with worn-out tires. If I pointed them out to you on the street, you would never believe they had any money. They earned every dime, and they're darn proud of it.

You're Never Too Old to Start

Most people in their 40s think it's too late to build wealth. They claim they don't have the energy they once had. They feel as if their peak earnings potential is behind them. They've missed out on too many opportunities. My response to these people is simply, "What about Anne Scheiver?"

Frank Lalli wrote an article about Anne Scheiver in *Money Magazine* ("How She Turned $5,000 into $22 Million," p. 64, January 1996, *Money*, Copyright 1996 Time, Inc.) that I found to be priceless. It read

> *In the depths of the Depression, when she was already 38 years old and earning only a little more than $3,000 a year, Anne invested a major portion of her life savings in stocks. She entrusted the money to the youngest of her four brothers, Bernard, who was getting started at 22 as a Wall Street broker. He did well picking issues for her as the market drifted upward in 1933 and '34, but his firm did not. It went bust suddenly, and Anne lost all her money. In 1944, 10 years after her big loss, she started*

fresh with a $5,000 account at Merrill Lynch Pierce Fenner & Bean and slowly built the nest egg up to $20 million by the time she died last January, loveless and alone at 101. It's now worth $22 million.

The article stated that her performance of 17.5 percent per year exceeded some of the best-known investment professionals in the world, including John Neff and Ben Graham. In 51 years, this incredible lady built a fortune using simple strategies that anyone can follow.

Wealth Warning

In spite of the fact that the chances of winning the lottery are usually worse than a million to one, it seems that most Americans use lottery tickets to plan for their retirement. The irony is that a large percentage of people who win the lottery end up in serious trouble, if not dead broke.

Investing with Passion

Those who knew Anne Scheiver said she lived a terrible existence as a recluse who never enjoyed her money. My bet is that investing was her passion, her love, and her life. I'm also willing to bet that this woman enjoyed her money more than most people ever will. She enjoyed managing it, not spending it. As a result, she turned near-disaster into an almost unbelievable fortune with nothing more than patience, interest in the market, research, and a little planning. So what if she didn't take vacations or eat out! This woman left a legacy behind that all of us can learn from. She was able to outperform trained professionals in their own field for more than 50 years. The story of Anne's life is what I call an invisible rags-to-riches story.

The Wealthy Postman

Here is a true story from which everyone can learn something; I know I did. The story involves a modest couple who attended my investment workshop in 1993. This couple, let's call them Mr. and Mrs. Post, met with me after the workshop to discuss some specific questions they had regarding their *no-load* fund portfolio. As usual, I asked some questions and found that Mr. Post had worked all his life for the United States Postal Service and was considering retirement the next year. His wife raised their children and had never earned any additional income. Mr. Post told me that the most they had ever made in one year was $30,000. They were conservatively dressed, simple in their ways, and almost shy about talking to me.

They wanted me to review their no-load mutual fund portfolio to see if I thought anything needed to be sold. As Mr. Post began to show me his portfolio, I put my pen down and prepared to see a small portfolio of funds.

Wrong! Their portfolio had more than 35 different no-load mutual funds worth more than $800,000. To say the least, I was dumbfounded. How could this couple have so much money? Well, of course, I made all kinds of assumptions. First, I asked if any of the money was inherited. They replied quickly and firmly, "No, not one dime." I asked if they owned any real estate other than their home. They replied, "No." I was impressed.

Words of the Wealthy

No-load funds are mutual funds that can be purchased, sold, and owned without any commission charges (or loads). The only charges involved are yearly management fees. A commission-paid broker or salesperson would never offer to sell you a no-load fund because there is no commission available for him.

They quickly told me that they had also purchased homes for each of their two daughters as wedding presents, both of which cost $120,000. They paid cash, of course. They had also prefunded their four grandchildren's college education with a total of $100,000. If you add that up, the total is $1,140,000. I gave up and asked how they did it. They came to me for advice, and I turned the appointment around and asked for theirs. What I learned from them that day I will never forget. This couple told me later in the most humble tone, "If we can do it, anybody can." They were invisibly wealthy.

That Reminds Me...

I've learned over the last 12 years in the wealth-management business that most of the really wealthy people do not own fancy cars, jet planes, or huge mansions. Most of the wealthy people I know are more like Sam Walton. They drive older cars or trucks, fly coach seats on commercial airlines, and wear simple clothes. To my surprise, most of them live well within their means in simple homes. They tend to avoid anything flashy and avoid large mortgages and car payments by paying cash. My point is that you would never think these people had any more money than the average citizen. As a matter of fact, they keep their wealth confidential.

Is a College Education Necessary?

Contrary to popular belief, a college education is not necessary for you to build great wealth. The world is full of super-intelligent people who never built any significant amount of wealth. What may surprise you is that many wealthy people never finished college.

Treasure Tip

No matter what your education or resources, the key to building financial wealth is to compose and follow a plan of action you design to meet your specific needs and goals. Your plan should identify and combat your weaknesses.

My second favorite story about wealthy people is about a man who built a $10 million net worth from the ground up without a college education. He worked hard and earned his net wealth. He decided to retire last year in his early 50s.

When he was 18, he decided to skip college and work in a soft drink distribution company. He was dedicated and worked harder than anyone in the company. In fact, he worked so hard that a truck driver at the company once told him, "Don't work so hard. You'll make all of us look bad." This didn't even faze him. He soon became a truck driver and then a supervisor for all the truck drivers.

After four years, a national soft drink company saw what he had done for his employer and asked him to be a division manager. This position gave him the opportunity to help other soft drink distributors in several states. In only a few years, one of his distributors offered him 20 percent of the company to manage his distributorship. He agreed, and they soon bought other distributorships and added other brands to their line. The original owner wanted to retire, so he offered the remaining stock to my client. The transaction involved a lot of money for my client at that time, so he took on a partner to make the transaction. Soon, they bought other distributorships in five states, including Hawaii.

The business became larger than my client ever dreamed. I asked him to sum it up in a few sentences how he built his wealth. He said, "Dedication, hard work, and going that extra mile." I asked him where he got his motivation to work so hard. He replied, "Believe it or not, it had a lot to do with the fact that I didn't have a college education. I felt like everyone else did, and I had this complex about not finishing college."

I really believe that a college education is a great idea, but it certainly is not a requirement for building wealth. My client proved that determination, hard work, and the willingness to go that extra mile are more important than a college education. By the way, the truck driver who told him to not work so hard is still a truck driver. I bet my client's wealth isn't invisible to him.

The Rich Couple Next Door

One day, a retired couple in their 60s came to my office for some help. They were a tiny couple, both about 5 feet tall, and wore clothes that had to be 10 years old. You couldn't ask for a nicer couple. They asked almost bashfully if I would take a look at their "little" portfolio and make some suggestions. They both apologized for the "small" size of their holdings. The husband said, "I know that you are accustomed to dealing with much larger amounts, but would you please give us some advice?" I explained that size didn't matter and that I would be glad to help them in any way I could. I nearly fell out of my chair when I opened the portfolio to find more than$1 million in stocks, bonds, and mutual funds. You would never think that these people had any money. It never ceases to amaze me how people such as this can be so humble and simple, yet be completely sophisticated with their investment knowledge.

I asked them a little about their background. They said that the most they ever made in income in one year was $27,000 and that they didn't inherit anything. I just love these people! I'm willing to bet that you know people just like this in your neighborhood, church, or synagogue. They are the salt of the earth, and if you can ever get them to tell you their story, you may learn more than you ever thought you could from these people.

That Reminds Me...

While working at a national discount brokerage firm, my associate Sharon Kolb got to know many wealthy people who earned their money from non-glamour businesses such as scrap metal salvage, electrical supply companies, used car lots, and other such endeavors. Sharon said, "It's really true that you don't need a formal education or work in a glamour field to earn a good living and build wealth."

Wealth and Adversity

It's strange how adversity can change the life of a person for the better. I've heard it said that the strongest pine lumber comes from trees that have been subject to windy environments. The same is true for people. The strongest people I know have struggled the most in life. Some of the wealthiest people I know have done the same. The difference between them and most people is their perseverance. The value of courage, persistence, and perseverance has rarely been illustrated more convincingly than in the life story of this man.

Event	Age
Failed in business	22
Ran for legislature—defeated	23
Again failed in business	24
Elected to legislature	25
Sweetheart died	26
Had a nervous breakdown	27
Defeated for speaker	29
Defeated for elector	31
Defeated for Congress	34
Elected to Congress	37
Defeated for Congress	39
Defeated for Senate	46
Defeated for Vice President	47
Defeated for Senate	49
Elected President of the United States	51

That's the record of Abraham Lincoln.

Don't Be a Hodad!

Just because someone makes a lot of money, it doesn't mean they're wealthy. If their expenses equal or exceed their income, they don't qualify as wealthy. Just because someone works hard, earns a great salary, and has nice things, it doesn't make him or her wealthy. The person may look like wealth and smell like wealth, but it's all a big show.

In Texas, they call these people *hodads*. They're all hat and no cattle. They wear fancy hats and talk the talk, but they don't even have a pasture or a cow to put in it.

Somewhere along the way, these seemingly wealthy people didn't learn the habits and characteristics necessary to build real wealth. No one taught them the concept of saving for a rainy day, much less retirement. They don't have what it takes to be wealthy.

Words of the Wealthy

Hodad is word used to describe people who are generally fake or phony. They may look like they're rich, they might smell like they're rich, but if you take a close look, you'll find they owe a lot of money and lease everything they have.

That Reminds Me...

I knew a business owner once who didn't have any capital, so he leased every single thing in his business. He leased his car, his condo, his office furniture, his office equipment, his office, and all his manufacturing equipment. Leases typically are ridiculously expensive, and therefore, he didn't make enough money for his business to survive, so he returned all his leased items, moved out of that industry, and went to another state. For a while there, he looked like a rich young man. Almost every guy in town envied him. He looked rich, but after a closer look, you could tell he was a hodad.

The Wealth Quiz

I know what you're saying, "So Larry, how do I become wealthy?" Most everyone I know would like to be rich. They may not all be willing to admit it, but it's the truth. If this is the case, then why do so few people get rich? What do these people do to become so wealthy? Why can't everyone do that? We are going to discuss the answers to all these questions throughout this book, but first, we must ask the most important question.

Do You Have What It Takes to Be Rich?

Let's see if you do. I have designed a test based solely on my own experience and the experiences of wealthy people I have met. Almost all of them share certain habits and characteristics. This test is not scientifically perfect, but the scoring levels measure your probability of achieving wealth.

The purpose of the wealth test is to get a picture of yourself today based upon what you have learned in the past and what you are doing now to achieve wealth. If you answer honestly, you will see what your chances would have been if you hadn't purchased this book and made the necessary adjustments. You don't have to show your results to anyone. Remember, your chances will increase once you've finished the book and implemented what you've learned. For now, let's focus on the "old you," and after the test, we'll focus on the "new you."

The Wealth Quiz

1.	Do you enjoy your work?	Yes	No
2.	Do you often visualize yourself achieving something bigger than what you are currently doing?	Yes	No
3.	Do you save money every month?	Yes	No
4.	Do you invest at least some of your money directly in the stock market either through a 401(k), individual stocks, or mutual funds?	Yes	No
5.	Do you shop before you buy most of the time, especially for big-ticket items?	Yes	No
6.	Do you take care of your home or apartment, performing regular maintenance as well as repairs?	Yes	No
7.	Do you perform regular maintenance on your car and other expensive items?	Yes	No
8.	Do you pay off the full balance on your credit cards each month?	Yes	No
9.	Are you comfortable buying used big-ticket items such as cars and appliances?	Yes	No
10.	Have you ever started your own business? (Even a lemonade stand counts.)	Yes	No
11.	Have you ever estimated how much money you would need in a portfolio to produce enough income to cover your current living expenses?	Yes	No

12. Do you measure the performance results of your portfolio at least yearly? Yes No
13. Do you maximize your personal contribution to your IRA or company's 401(k) plan? Yes No
14. Is your mortgage payment less than 20 percent of your total gross household income? (If you do not own a home, is your rent less than 20 percent of your total gross household income?) Yes No
15. Do you spend less than you make? Yes No
16. Have you ever read a book about building wealth or an autobiography about someone who was wealthy? Yes No
17. Do you have your own business now that produces a positive net income? Yes No
18. Have you ever worked all night or more than 24 hours on a project? Yes No

For each question that you answered yes, give yourself one point.

Total these points and then compare the total to the scale below to check the probability of becoming wealthy.

Score	Probability of Becoming Rich
1–5	Low
6–10	Average
11–15	Very likely
16–18	You are on your way!

Even if you scored low on the test, don't worry about it. A low score simply means that if you don't change some things in your life, the probability of becoming wealthy is low. All you have to do is be willing to make some changes. Regardless of your score, you can achieve wealth. Your score just identifies your weak points. Take a moment and look at the questions to which you answered "No."

These are your areas of weakness. By identifying these areas now, you will recognize the solutions as you study this book. They reflect the areas that you need to change.

Why Are Most People Not Wealthy?

Why is it so difficult to get rich? Most people lack the willingness to change their ways. Building wealth is a way of life. It's a mindset or paradigm that few people are willing to accept. Achieving the mindset often requires only a few simple changes in the way we think about and view life.

> **Wealth Warning**
>
> Two other common ways to become wealthy include inheritance and marriage. Most people who achieve wealth in that manner do not become good stewards of their money.

Most people also lack the discipline to maintain the changes. It's not easy to change, much less make the change permanent. Most people don't have the tenacity or "stick-to-it-ness" necessary to build wealth. They give up too easily.

Brian Tracy, in his famous cassette tape series, "The Psychology of Achievement," mentioned a study that was done several years ago involving a group of people who were worth more than $1 million before the age of 30. They were all asked, "How many different businesses were you involved in before you became a millionaire?" The average answer was 18. Can you imagine? What does this tell you? It tells me that achieving wealth takes a heck of a lot of tenacity and patience. You have to be willing to stick to this goal and be willing to fail more than once. I speak from experience. When I don't enjoy what I'm doing, the chances are good that I'm going to give up after failing the first few times. My money-management firm lost money during the first three years of business, but this didn't get me down. I had a passion for building my firm that would never let me quit. Now, my profit margin exceeds 50 percent.

> **That Reminds Me...**
>
> Motivation and accomplishment can come from adversity. The first company I worked for just out of college did not pay me bonuses I earned. When I quit, my boss yelled, "You're a quitter, a loser. You'll never get a job anywhere. You'll never achieve anything." This motivated me. All I could think about was making enough money one day to buy the company and have him work for me. Quitting enabled me to go into the investment industry—my true passion. I have no interest in buying that company any more. Maybe I should thank the guy for motivating me so much at an early age.

The Misconceptions of Wealth

Now that I've seen both sides of the story, I've learned that there are many misconceptions regarding wealth. People simply misunderstand what wealth is and how you get it. It may sound simple, but it's the truth. I've seen it all my life. I remember that growing up as a child, I heard people make hundreds of comments about their concept of wealth. These misconceptions may hold these people back from wealth for the rest of their lives. If you hold any of these misconceptions, one of the things you should do immediately is stop using them as an excuse not to build your wealth. Here are a few of the most common misconceptions. I call them the fallacies of wealth:

- If I had a lot of money, my problems would go away.
- It would be easy to decide how to spend my money and whom to leave it to.
- More people will like me if I am more successful.
- Getting rich is something that only happens to other people.
- If I just had a little more money, I'd be happy.
- If I were wealthy, I could buy anything I want.
- I wish I were wealthy so I wouldn't have to worry about money anymore.
- I'm young; I've got plenty of time to become wealthy. Why save money now?
- I'm too old to start saving money.
- I wish I had saved more money when I was younger.
- There's no chance of me ever becoming wealthy. I only make $20,000 a year.
- The only way to get rich is inheriting the money, winning the lottery, owning commercial real estate, or starting a business.
- If I were really wealthy, I wouldn't care how much I paid in taxes.

I think it all boils down to one thing: Most people aren't willing to make the decisions or sacrifice it takes to become wealthy. The whole process seems too overwhelming to them. Admittedly, if you are starting with little or no money, this process of building wealth might seem overwhelming. *But it's not impossible!* If you think becoming wealthy is impossible, well, you can bet it will be. You'll never make it. Someone once said, "Argue your limitations and they're yours." Therefore, if you want to get rich, stop arguing your limitations and get busy.

Wealth Is a Journey

Building wealth is basically a lifestyle change, just like losing weight or starting a new hobby. It's a journey, not a destination. We change our lives by changing our attitudes and perceptions. Whether you believe you *can* or you *can't*—you're right. In the end, we become exactly what we think about. If you think about what you lack, you will always lack. If you have an attitude of abundance, you will have abundance.

You will often get trapped in a comfort zone that could ultimately stalemate your efforts. Remember to be aware of these zones and don't get too comfortable. Don't be afraid of making mistakes. Mistakes will teach you everything you need to know if you're willing to learn from them.

That Reminds Me...

Every year, I ask my associates to give me three answers to this question: What one great thing would you dare to attempt if you knew you could not fail? My associate Angie Johnson said that she wanted to run a full marathon (26 miles). She ran a little almost everyday but had never gone beyond 5 miles at that time. Less than a year later, she ran her first marathon in 3 hours and 50 minutes. She worked very hard, never gave up, and sacrificed a lot of time to train for the event. Who knows what she'll be doing next!

Occasionally, you'll have setbacks. You can plan for most of them in advance. However, if you do fall back, all you have to do is retrace your steps and continue your journey. Remember that wealth is a journey and not a destination. When you make the decision to seek wealth, you have taken the first step on a life-long journey. Let's get started.

The Least You Need to Know

- Wealth can be built by anyone at any age who is willing to learn and develop the habits and characteristics necessary.
- The habits and characteristics are simple to understand and easy to implement but grossly overlooked by so many people.
- Start identifying the common misconceptions of wealth, and don't let them hold you back from achieving your fortune.
- To build real wealth, you have to believe that it can be done.
- Wealth is a journey that requires a high level of tenacity and determination to overcome the occasional setbacks.

Chapter 2

Eleven Tools for Building Wealth

In This Chapter

- How to think like an investor
- Using the enormous power of time
- Compound growth—the eighth wonder of the world
- Using debt as a tool
- What is net worth?

Before you start any project, you must know what tools to use and how to use them. Once you know the proper tools and how they work together, the project is much easier to finish. This chapter will teach you the basic tools you need to build wealth. These tools are easy to understand and easy to use. Every industry has its own unique language, which consists of the jargon and concepts that are used every day. Because almost everyone deals with at least some financial issues, most of the terms should already be somewhat familiar. Even so, it's important to make sure that we are all using the same language for our discussions.

The concept of wealth is unique for everyone. Each person has his own definition that may or may not emphasize financial wealth. As you know, for the purpose of this book, we are focusing on financial wealth. The tools discussed in this chapter are specifically for building financial wealth.

Tools to Build Your Wealth

Before discussing the specific definition of wealth in the next chapter, let's go over the 11 necessary tools for building wealth:

1. Investments
2. Time
3. Compounding growth
4. Living expenses
5. Risk management
6. Inflation awareness
7. Taxes minimization
8. Debt
9. Target savings goal (TSG)
10. Salary or income
11. Net worth

If you don't understand these tools, you will have trouble understanding the logic of the next chapter.

Investments

An investment is something you can buy that has the potential of returning to you more money than you spent to buy it originally. Therefore, before you buy an investment, you have to think like an investor. Your biggest concern should be the amount of money you'll get back in the future from the investment. The second biggest concern should be the risk of volatility in the investment's value while holding it. Will the price fluctuate over time? Can you handle that? What's the risk of the investment becoming worthless? When you make a decision to buy an investment, these are the questions to ask.

For the purpose of this material, the term investments primarily refers to *liquid assets*, which are

Words of the Wealthy

An asset can be liquid or illiquid property that can be sold for cash. This can include stocks, bonds, and real estate. **Liquid assets** include those assets that can be instantly converted into cash. **Illiquid assets** are just the opposite; they are not easily converted into cash.

securities that are traded in a regulated market such as the banking or stock markets. An asset is considered liquid if it can be easily sold for cash within an established financial market. This includes stocks, bonds, CDs (certificates of deposit), mutual funds, and foreign securities. The most common liquid assets are checking and money market accounts. You can sell or liquidate these assets and get your money within 24 hours.

A portfolio could also include *illiquid assets* such as privately held securities or commercial real estate. These assets are not easily sold for cash because you have to find a buyer yourself. However, there is absolutely nothing wrong with illiquid assets. For example, the most commonly held illiquid asset is a home. It can be sold and converted to cash, but the process can take some time. Another example of an illiquid asset is privately held stock (which is not listed on an exchange such as the New York Stock Exchange).

What's the problem with owning illiquid assets? Establishing a price tag. Illiquid assets are not always easy to value. Therefore, they must be evaluated by an expert to establish a fair market value.

Many wealthy people have built their fortunes using illiquid assets such as land, commercial buildings, and *privately held company* stock. However, these people understood the characteristics and risks unique to each particular illiquid asset. Do not attempt to get involved with illiquid assets without doing some serious homework. If you understand what you own and the market you participate in, you can make money by investing in illiquid assets.

Words of the Wealthy

A **privately held company** is one in which its shares are not publicly traded. Privately held stock is issued to a small number of shareholders, and the value or price of the stock is usually determined by comparisons with other similar companies using factors such as company earnings and gross income.

The Value of Time

Most people don't realize the value of time and its effect on an investment. Time is a powerful tool. If you are in your 20s or 30s, you have an advantage over someone in her 40s or 50s. When I think of the time component, I think of an old expression, "Give me a lever long enough and I can move the world." Time works the same way with wealth. Give me enough time and I can build a fortune. The opposite is also true. The less time you have, the less likely it is that you will build any significant

> **Wealth Warning**
>
> The tool of time can also work in reverse. The longer you wait to start your portfolio, the harder it is to build any significant wealth. A good place to start your investment portfolio is a $2,000 IRA, which can grow tax deferred until all the money is drawn out during retirement. This account allows you to combine the tools of time, compound growth, and tax deferral.

wealth. It's not impossible, however, to use this tool later in life. Remember Anne Scheiver in the first chapter, who began saving at the age of 50 and died with a $20 million portfolio. If she can do it, so can you.

Let's take a closer look at how important time is in the accumulation of wealth. The following table illustrates the progress of a portfolio for an early saver versus a portfolio for someone who starts saving later.

The Early Saver Versus the Late Saver

Age	Early Start			Late Start		
22	$2,000	$180	$2,180	$0	$0	$0
23	$2,000	$376	$4,556	$0	$0	$0
24	$2,000	$590	$7,146	$0	$0	$0
25	$2,000	$823	$9,969	$0	$0	$0
26	$2,000	$1,077	$13,047	$0	$0	$0
27	$2,000	$1,354	$16,401	$0	$0	$0
28	$2,000	$1,656	$20,057	$0	$0	$0
29	$2,000	$1,985	$24,042	$0	$0	$0
30	$2,000	$2,344	$28,386	$0	$0	$0
31	$0	$2,555	$30,941	$2,000	$180	$2,180
32	$0	$2,785	$33,725	$2,000	$376	$4,556
33	$0	$3,035	$36,761	$2,000	$590	$7,146
34	$0	$3,308	$40,069	$2,000	$823	$9,969
35	$0	$3,606	$43,675	$2,000	$1,077	$13,047
36	$0	$3,931	$47,606	$2,000	$1,354	$16,401
37	$0	$4,285	$51,890	$2,000	$1,656	$20,057
38	$0	$4,670	$56,561	$2,000	$1,985	$24,042

Age	Early Start			Late Start		
39	$0	$5,090	$61,651	$2,000	$2,344	$28,386
40	$0	$5,549	$67,200	$2,000	$2,735	$33,121
41	$0	$6,048	$73,248	$2,000	$3,161	$38,281
42	$0	$6,592	$79,840	$2,000	$3,625	$43,907
43	$0	$7,186	$87,025	$2,000	$4,132	$50,038
44	$0	$7,832	$94,858	$2,000	$4,683	$56,722
45	$0	$8,537	$103,395	$2,000	$5,285	$64,007
46	$0	$9,306	$112,701	$2,000	$5,941	$71,947
47	$0	$10,143	$122,844	$2,000	$6,655	$80,603
48	$0	$11,056	$133,900	$2,000	$7,434	$90,037
49	$0	$12,051	$145,950	$2,000	$8,283	$100,320
50	$0	$13,136	$159,086	$2,000	$9,209	$111,529
51	$0	$14,318	$173,404	$2,000	$10,218	$123,747
52	$0	$15,606	$189,010	$2,000	$11,317	$137,064
53	$0	$17,011	$206,021	$2,000	$12,516	$151,580
54	$0	$18,542	$224,563	$2,000	$13,822	$167,402
55	$0	$20,211	$244,774	$2,000	$15,246	$184,648
56	$0	$22,030	$266,803	$2,000	$16,798	$203,446
57	$0	$24,012	$290,815	$2,000	$18,490	$223,936
58	$0	$26,173	$316,989	$2,000	$20,334	$246,271
59	$0	$28,529	$345,518	$2,000	$22,344	$270,615
60	$0	$31,097	$376,614	$2,000	$24,535	$297,150
61	$0	$33,895	$410,510	$2,000	$26,924	$326,074
62	$0	$36,946	$447,456	$2,000	$29,527	$357,601
63	$0	$40,271	$487,727	$2,000	$32,364	$391,965
64	$0	$43,895	$531,622	$2,000	$35,457	$429,422
65	$0	$47,846	$579,468	$2,000	$38,828	$470,249
Total Deposited by Each: $18,000				**$70,000**		

**Please note that this illustration is for comparison purposes only.*

**Taxes are not calculated into the equation.*

The first investor deposits $18,000 between the ages of 22 and 30 and ends up with a $579,468 account. The second investor gets a later start and deposits $70,000 between the ages of 31 and 65— almost four times as much money—but his account grows to only $470,249. That's a difference of $109,219. How is this possible? The first investor simply had the advantage of more time to compound the growth. Notice that by the time the second investor began saving money, the first investor's gain exceeded the second investor's deposit. Time is powerful stuff and is often completely overlooked. Use the power of time.

Words of the Wealthy

Total return, also known as portfolio performance, refers to the percentage return of an investment or portfolio that includes dividends, interest, and capital gains. By the way, when the total return is reinvested into the investment or portfolio, the result is compound growth.

Time is also important during times of volatility. In a bear market, many investors lose sight of the value of time, and they focus on the short term and not the long term.

Compound Growth

Compound growth is different from compound interest. It is achieved when you invest in stocks (or anything that appreciates in value) over a long period of time while allowing the capital gains and dividends to reinvest into the original investment. The combination of your dividends, interest, and capital gains is also known as *total return*.

Over the past seven years, I have spoken to more than two thousand investors—both successful and unsuccessful. What idea seems to be common among those who are successful is simple: Successful investors understand that compound growth is the most powerful investment tool—second only to research.

Treasure Tip

Dr. Albert Einstein left Germany to come to the United States to escape potential conflict with Hitler. It has been said that a young reporter met Einstein when he arrived at the Port of New York and asked him what he believed was the eighth wonder of the world. Einstein replied, "I believe it is compound interest."

What makes compound growth so attractive is the added effect of price appreciation with reinvested interest or dividends.

The next concept is the total return on your capital. Total return consists of dividends, interest, and capital gains. A capital gain is the price appreciation realized from the sale of an asset. If you invest in real estate, your portfolio might also produce rental income. Total return is also known as portfolio gains, portfolio performance, and portfolio growth.

The most confusing concept about total return involves taking regular monthly income from your portfolio, which is most commonly necessary once retirement begins. When taking income from a liquid portfolio for living expenses, most investors look only at dividends and interest (cash flow). They pay little, if any, attention to capital gain because they claim it's not reliable. This is conventional thinking.

In the long run, capital gains can be reliable from a properly diversified portfolio. Whether you are building wealth in the early years or maintaining wealth in the later years, you should not ignore capital gains. You should harvest them over time and consider them part of the cash flow. This unconventional concept of *harvesting* might be new to you; that's okay. To build and maintain the levels of wealth this book discusses, you must think unconventionally.

Words of the Wealthy

Harvesting is a term I use to describe a more unconventional method of deriving income that includes not only dividends and interest, but also capital gains. You can easily obtain capital gains occasionally selling (harvesting) pieces of a portfolio that have appreciated.

That Reminds Me...

The rule of 72 estimates how fast money can compound over time. Divide the number 72 by the rate of return you expect to receive. The result is the number of years it will take for your money to double. If you get 6 percent, your money would double in 12 years. If you get 8 percent, your money would double in 9 years; if 10 percent, 7.2 years; if 12 percent, 6 years. It also works in reverse. Divide the number 72 by the number of years you have to invest. The result is the percentage of total return you need to double the portfolio. This equation measures pure compound growth without the effect of any taxes. Therefore, it works best in measuring the growth of tax deferred accounts such as 401(k)s and qualified plans.

Wealth Warning

Ignoring your spending habits relative to your income will quickly get you into hot water.

Wealth Warning

You must be willing to make some sacrifices now to build wealth in the future.

Living Expenses

There are many different categories of expenses. Variable expenses cover entertainment, clothing, and travel. Fixed expenses are rent or mortgage payments. Living expenses might seem like a relatively boring subject, but most people don't understand just how important the expense component can be in building wealth. When you are just beginning to build your portfolio, the amount of money you spend monthly for expenses directly affects the speed of your journey to wealth. If you are accustomed to a high standard of living with no willingness to be flexible, your chances of saving money in the early years are small.

I truly believe that the main reason people don't save money is that they are unwilling to limit their standard of living. I mostly see this unwillingness in young couples but also notice it in older retired couples. In the later years, especially during retirement, if you spend more than your portfolio produces, you deplete your capital source or principal. I now have a client who started with a $100,000 retirement account. For the past two years, this client has lived beyond his means, and the account is now worth only $33,000. His portfolio grew faster than the world stock market index but didn't grow fast enough to keep up with his spending habits. This scenario is a nightmare that didn't have to happen. The client did not measure spending habits, ignored his resources, and now has a big problem. Don't let this scenario happen to you. It's important to understand that systematic measurement of your monthly expenses is vital to the wealth-building process. (I show you how to do this in Chapter 3, "The Five Stages of Wealth.")

Risk Management

I discuss the many different types of risk in more detail later. For our purposes in this chapter, the two basic types of risk are portfolio and situational. Portfolio risk can be defined as the volatility (the potential to rise or fall quickly) of the total portfolio value. Some investors are willing to accept higher levels of volatility for higher rates of return. Return is your reward for your willingness to assume risk. In general, risk can increase your potential for return, but it can also lead to more potential for loss. Setting proper return goals involves determining your acceptable level of risk.

Situational risk is the chance you'll experience health problems, premature death, a disability, an automobile accident, or another liability. Each of these risks has the potential of ruining your journey toward building serious financial wealth. However, you can manage each of these risks using the right insurance tool. A wealthy person understands these risks and manages each type efficiently using the right insurance tools. Therefore, insurance is also an important tool.

Wealth Warning

Risk tolerance is the degree to which an investor can live with the volatility of his or her portfolio. When asked, most investors tend to overestimate their tolerance for risk. However, when confronted with significantly poor performance or losses from an investment, they fully understand their true tolerance.

Inflation Awareness

Inflation is what happens when too many dollars chase too little goods. It takes place when the economy is growing strong, wages are high, and consumers are spending a lot of money. For example, during a time of increased consumer spending, retailers can easily raise prices a little without bothering the consumer much. The opposite is also true. If the economy is not growing strongly, wages are low, and consumers are not spending a lot of money, then retailers may have to drop prices. This situation is called disinflation.

Inflation is simply an increase in the price of goods and services. The most important thing to remember about inflation is that it will affect your future living expenses. I remember 10 cent sodas and 25 cent hamburgers. What costs a dollar today may cost five dollars in the future. You must take inflation into account when making projections about the future. The easy way to measure and project inflation is to use the Consumer Price Index (CPI), which is the yearly growth rate of the total price of a basket of consumer goods. All financial publications show this rate as the CPI. It isn't a perfect measurement, but most economists use it. You will need to know this index in Chapter 3 when I show you how to project your future living expenses.

That Reminds Me...

Tabulated by the U.S. Government's Bureau of Labor Statistics, the CPI measures the cost of a representative basket of consumer goods, which might include a loaf of bread, a gallon of milk, or a hamburger. The price of the basket is not that important. The most important aspect of CPI is the rate of change from one month to another. The amount of change from month to month in the cost of this basket of goods is stated as a percentage of the CPI for the previous month. This percentage is known as the rate of inflation and is usually quoted as an annualized percentage. This measurement appears in the *Wall Street Journal* in Section A at approximately the middle of the month.

Taxes Minimization

When I mention taxes, I am referring to all federal, state, and local income taxes. Specifically, in the next chapter, you will need to know your overall income tax rate. An easy way to calculate this is to add up the federal, state, and local taxes you paid last year and divide that amount by your gross income. This will give you your income tax rate. If you need help calculating this, ask your CPA.

> (Federal + State + Local Taxes) ÷ Gross Annual Income = Your Income Tax Rate

For example, if you had a gross income of $30,000 with federal taxes of $3,540 and state taxes of $1,344, your average income tax rate equals 16.28 percent.

Taxes can be avoided or deferred using certain investment vehicles. However, the most important goal of an investor should be to make money, not avoid taxes. If you focus primarily on avoiding taxes, you might accomplish your goal, but I can promise you that you will not make much money in the process.

Debt

Debt is simply a loan, which can include a home mortgage, personal loans, business loans, and lines of credit. Don't get me wrong: Debt can be a big problem in the wealth-building process. However, it can also be a great tool. If you want to build serious wealth, you need a good relationship with a banker who can service your needs properly. The most common healthy debt tools include a home mortgage, business loans, and lines of credit. All of these tools can help you leverage your wealth (or cash flow) in order to afford a home, invest in a business, or cushion cash-flow problems.

I do not recommend the use of margin in an investment account. A margin loan is simply a loan against the securities in your account. I also do not recommend loans for purchases that improve your self-image, such as fancy cars and boats. My hope is that this book helps you look at everything you buy, especially when you borrow money to buy it, as an investment. As I said previously, your biggest concern is the amount of money you'll get back in the future from the investment. The risk gets worse if you get *upside down*. You're upside down when you borrow money to buy something, and it falls in value so much that the money you owe exceeds the value of the item.

Words of the Wealthy

You're **upside down** when you borrow money to buy a car and the value of the car drops below the total value of the loan.

Target Savings Goal

An important concept for building wealth is the amount of money you save every month or every year. The two terms I use are *target savings goal (TSG)* and actual savings. Your target savings goal (TSG) is the amount of money you need to save every year in order to build a portfolio large enough to produce a total return by a certain date (usually retirement) that will sustain your standard of living plus keep up with inflation. I realize that this definition might be a mouthful, but, don't worry, it's simpler than it seems. I discuss this concept step-by-step in Chapter 4 and make it easy for you.

Words of the Wealthy

Your **target savings goal,** or **TSG,** refers to the amount of money required each year to build a portfolio large enough to support your preferred standard of living at retirement.

Your actual savings amount is just what it says: the difference between your total household income and expenses. This surplus is what goes into your investment account. If there is money available for savings, you are living within your means and that's great. If you have a negative actual savings amount, you are living beyond your means, and that's not good at all.

The actual savings amount is important in the early stages of your life. Therefore, your focus should be on saving and investing as much as you can when you are young. During the first years of saving when your portfolio is small, total return is relatively less important than the amount of money you save (the deposits you make). The deposits you make at first will dwarf the amount of money you make on your investments (the dividends and gains). Therefore, your early years of saving is a great time to learn about investing. When you are new to the game of investing, you tend to make a lot of mistakes. If you can make those mistakes early, when the returns have less effect on your overall portfolio, you save your portfolio from harm later when your return really counts.

Salary or Income

Before you can save any money, you have to be making money, which most people refer to as cash flow. The most common source of cash flow is a salary. The idea is that you spend less than your salary so that after taxes, you have some excess cash flow to save and invest. Your salary is a key tool in the wealth-building process.

Treasure Tip

Compound interest refers to fixed income investments where interest is earned and reinvested causing a compounding effect. Compound growth is different in that it refers to stocks and other investments that appreciate in value causing a potentially faster compounding effect. Compound growth over time allows even moderate rates of return to produce great wealth.

Most people believe that your salary is the most important tool. The bigger the salary, the more you have to spend and invest. This is certainly true. However, many people get caught up more in the spending rather than the investing. Increasing your salary is wonderful for the wealth-building process if you can discipline yourself to save more as you make more. As I've illustrated for you in the last chapter, a hefty salary is not necessary to build significant wealth. Don't get discouraged if your salary isn't as high as you want it to be. By all means, do what you can to maximize your salary, but don't get so caught up that you lose sight of other tools such as compound growth, time, and controlling expenses.

Net Worth

The definition of net worth is the value of your assets and investments minus your debt or liabilities:

Assets – Liabilities = Net Worth

The idea is to increase assets and decrease liabilities. In reality, you may find yourself increasing liabilities temporarily in order to increase assets at a future date. The key is to focus on assets that grow over time. The most powerful asset to own is usually stock in your own business. The second most powerful tool is stock in someone else's busines.

The Least You Need to Know

- To build significant wealth, think like an investor and focus on the amount of money you'll get back from your investment in the future.
- The more time you allow your portfolio to compound its growth, the more potential you have to build significant wealth.
- The eighth wonder of the world is considered compound interest, which requires you to maintain a long-term view with your investments.
- If you are accustomed to a high standard of living with no willingness to be flexible, your chances of saving money in the early years are small.
- You must understand and manage both portfolio risk and situational risk in order to maintain your journey toward wealth.
- To build your net worth, your long-term focus should be increasing assets and decreasing liabilities.

Chapter 3

The Five Stages of Wealth

In This Chapter

- Calculating your current net worth
- How to calculate your stage of wealth
- What you should focus on when attempting to achieve each stage
- How to get through these stages faster
- When saving money becomes less important

Everyone's definition of financial wealth is different. To make things simple, I've defined five specific, measurable stages of wealth. These stages reduce the confusion surrounding the concept of wealth by breaking down the definition into easy-to-understand pieces.

The first thing you must realize in your search for a personal definition of wealth is that your definition will always be a relative term. Relative to what? A poor immigrant family might say that being rich means having an apartment with running water and a roof overhead. You might like to be wealthy relative to your neighbor or friend. I was guilty of this when I was a young man in my 20s. I found myself constantly in a battle to build more wealth than that of other people I knew. The only problem was that I constantly met new people who were wealthier than the last. The benchmark kept moving, and it always seemed out of reach. Your idea of wealth should be defined relative to your desired standard of living—not your neighbor's or your friend's. Be realistic about this standard, and focus on what income stage makes you happy. Your life will be a lot easier, and you will feel more fulfilled in the process.

To learn more about wealth, you must associate yourself with wealthy people. You can do this through clubs, non-profit organizations, church, and friends who can introduce you. An alternative is to read books about wealthy people. You need to learn how they think, how they got there, and what is important to them—their values.

What Is Your Net Worth?

The most common way to define your current stage of wealth is to measure your net worth. When you go to a bank and apply for a loan, one of the first things they want is a net worth statement. This statement lists both liquid and illiquid assets, subtracts your liabilities (debts you owe, such as your mortgage), and results in a bottom-line net worth amount. Take a moment and copy the following net worth statement. Fill it out and calculate your net worth today. Be sure to date it so you'll be able to look back and compare in the future.

Net Worth Statement

Assets	Total Value
Cash	________
Money market funds	________
Savings account	________
Real estate (estimated current market value)	________
Residence	________
Farm	________
Other	________
Investments	
Individual stocks	________
Individual bonds	________
Mutual funds	________
401(k)	________
IRA	________
Other retirement plans	________
Closely held business (estimated current market value)	________
Equity interest	________
Personal Assets	
Automobile	________
Jewelry	________
Other	________
Total Assets	________

Assets	Total Value
Liabilities	
Personal line of credit (short term)	________
Home mortgage(s)	________
Automobile loan(s)	________
Other	________
Total Liabilities	________
Net Worth (Total Assets Minus Total Liabilities)	________

Now that you understand the 11 key wealth concepts from Chapter 2, "Eleven Tools for Building Wealth," let's discuss the five stages of wealth. Please understand these stages are my definitions. Each person has his or her own definition of wealth, which might not involve anything financial. Wealth to one person might be extensive wisdom. Wealth to another might be artistic ability. This material focuses on financial wealth.

I have defined five stages of financial wealth; each stage is defined relative to your current or desired standard of living.

Wealth Stage 1

The beginning of your journey is Stage 1. At this stage, you are able to maintain your standard of living and save enough money to achieve your target savings goal. This stage is as easy to achieve as you make it. It usually involves only a simple mindset change. When you live within your means and your actual savings amount equals or exceeds your TSG, you've made it to Wealth Stage 1. It's the easiest stage to achieve and can be your wealth safeguard if you fail at other stages.

> **Wealth Warning**
>
> The attitude today in the U.S. seems to be "spend now, save later." Although Southeast Asians save more than 30 percent of their income, we only save about 4 percent. If this keeps up, we are going to have a serious problem.

Don't misunderstand: Wealth Stage 1 has nothing to do with looking wealthy or building a financially wealthy outer image. In fact, in many ways, it means to do just the opposite. If you really want to achieve Stage 1, you may have to simplify your life and reduce expenses in order to achieve your target savings goal. Building wealth is not about buying fancy cars and clothes. It's about living within your means. If you can't handle this concept, you'll never achieve significant wealth.

Most people would love to build wealth. However, many get caught up in the glamour and excitement of spending rather than saving. The end result is that they don't live within their means, and they never even make it to Stage 1.

The wealthy people I know each have a passion. They spend their time and energy focusing on what they're passionate about, which usually doesn't cost too much money.

Several of my favorite clients with net worths more than $1 million spend their time doing home-improvement projects. I don't mean just painting. These people redo entire bathrooms and kitchens themselves. They love it, and they make money when they sell the home.

You don't have to be a home-improvement expert to be wealthy. You just need to be aware of how you're spending your time and money. Could you be more productive with your time and still follow your passion? My passion is writing and teaching people how to build and maintain wealth. I can't think of many things that could be more fun. Does it cost a lot of money to do that? No! In fact, the only money I'm spending now is on the electric bill. I talk more in Chapter 5, "The Secrets of Millionaires," about how to find your passion and later how you might be able to make money with that passion.

Wealth Warning

Let's face it: Saving money is boring to most people. Commercial advertisements and our "give it to me now" society makes spending fun. To many people, shopping is an escape. Some people even use this experience to make them feel and look wealthy. Ironically, it takes more energy to shop and spend than it does to save money.

Treasure Tip

You don't need a college education to earn a high income, but it does help. According to Census Bureau surveys in 1993, less than 6 percent of U.S. households earn more than $100,000 per year, 68 percent of which are headed by college graduates. The median household income of college graduates is $55,000, which is 76 percent higher than the median income for all households.

What's Your Focus Here?

To make it to Wealth Stage 1, the most important thing is your actual savings amount. This will affect the portfolio much more than the compound growth on your portfolio. For now, compound growth is of secondary importance. The most common mistake made by neophyte investors is that they focus too much on compound growth. Consequently, many of them end up taking too much risk and losing their money. To achieve and maintain this stage, you should focus on maximizing your actual savings amount as much as you possibly can.

During your journey toward Wealth Stage 1, you should also focus on learning as much as you can about investment management and learn from your mistakes now. These mistakes, if made now, will not have nearly the effect they will later when your account is larger and the mistakes are harder to recover from. For example, a common mistake made by neophyte investors is the use of futures and options contracts, which is not a wise way to start investing. I know because I did it and lost a lot of money. However, I'm glad I did this in the early part of my life. It taught me early to stick with stocks, bonds, and mutual funds.

It may be easier to conquer Stage 1 in steps. For example, you could set your first target savings goal at 5 percent of your net monthly income. The second goal could be 10 percent; third, 15 percent; and so on. The last step is to save your true total TSG. If you save in slowly increasing amounts over time and continue this habit through life as your income increases, you will dramatically increase your chances of reaching Wealth Stages 2 through 5.

Setting and sticking to a savings goal may sound easy, but I know so few people who do. Most are unwilling to cut back their standard of living in order to save the 10 percent, or they are unwilling to try harder for more income. They procrastinate, never save any money, have too much pride to cut back their spending, borrow too much to keep up with the neighbors, or just never think about the future. Whatever the reason, they will never achieve the stage of wealth they desire.

Wealth Stage 2

At the beginning of Wealth Stage 2, your portfolio is large enough to produce, on its own, compound growth each year equal to your TSG. That means you have now, in essence, doubled your TSG: One part comes from your monthly TSG deposit and the other part from portfolio gains. You've really harnessed the power of compound growth. The combined effect of your TSG deposit and compound growth produces enormous portfolio growth power for you.

What's Your Focus Here?

Because at this stage your actual savings amount and compound growth are equal, they become equally important. You must focus on both components. This is also the stage of wealth where knowledge of risk becomes vital to the remainder of the wealth-building process. Unfortunately, most people wait until this stage to begin learning about risks. Bad investment decisions made in Wealth Stage 2 are more costly than they would have been in Stage 1.

You haven't completed Wealth Stage 2 when your portfolio's annual return equals your TSG. There are actually three steps to this stage. Stage 2 continues as your portfolio produces a compound growth equal to two times your TSG. Therefore, your portfolio is growing by three times your TSG. One part is your actual TSG deposit, and the other two parts come from portfolio performance. The most important component becomes compound growth. Your actual savings amount still helps speed the process, but compound growth is more important and powerful. If compound growth is twice the size of your actual savings amount, then your downside risk is also twice as big. This makes mistakes more difficult to recover from. Suddenly, compound growth becomes important, and therefore, making the right investment decisions becomes paramount. This certainly also makes risk management vital.

> **Wealth Warning**
>
> There are four categories of risks involving stocks: specific issue risk, which involves the risk of the individual company; industry risk, the company's industry; country risk, the risk of the country in which the company resides; and world risk, the risk of the world market.

You've reached the third step of Wealth Stage 2 when your portfolio produces a compound growth equal to three times your TSG. The compounding effect is expanding your portfolio three times faster than your own deposit. Now the relative effect of an additional deposit equal to your TSG has little influence on the growth of the portfolio. That doesn't mean you need to stop saving money! It just means that compound growth is vital, and investment management has never before been so important.

Wealth Stage 3

If your portfolio produces compound growth large enough to cover your desired lifestyle and inflation, then congratulations! You've made it to

Wealth Stage 3. Employment is optional, and your money is working hard for you. According to my research, only about 5 percent of the population achieve this stage of wealth by retirement age. Most of my clients have made it to this stage. They enjoy life and they have the option to work. They have more freedom to focus on what they love to do. Ironically, most of them don't retire at this point if they enjoy what they do. If they don't enjoy their work, they often make the changes necessary to get into what they do enjoy the most.

Wealth Warning

Our Social Security system has produced a population of citizens who believe in their right to a subsidized comfortable retirement. After seeing thousands of workers realize their benefits are much less than they expected, I came to the conclusion that my comfortable retirement depends on me and my efforts.

Retirement is only a transition into another passion. Once people make the decision to retire, or at least slow down, their living expenses usually decrease. Maybe they take more vacations and spend more money, but they still live within their means. The habit is so ingrained that they actually feel uncomfortable spending more than normal, even if they can afford it. My "retired" clients are like most wealthy people in the world. They built their wealth over a long period of time by living well within their means, and they maintain their wealth by continuing to do the same.

What's Your Focus Here?

The most important component in Wealth Stage 3 is compound growth. The amount of money you're saving is probably dwarfed by the effect of compound growth. Likewise, your potential downside is also significant, which reduces your ability to recover from a loss using additional deposits. Therefore, the second most important tool is risk. This is especially true if you are no longer earning a salary. If you're not comfortable managing your own portfolio when it's this large, you'd better get some help.

If you are relying upon your portfolio for income (such as to pay your living expenses after you retire), you have to focus on two components: compound growth and living expenses. If you spend more than your portfolio produces, over the long run, you'll erode your income-generating capital and drop back into Stage 1 or 2 with no source of income to replace what you lost. The wealthy people I know in this stage prevent this from happening by simply making it a habit to live well within their means. They always spend less than their total income.

Wealth Stage 4

You have accumulated enough assets to produce compound growth sufficient enough to substantially increase your desired lifestyle, while at the same time keep up with inflation. If you've made it beyond Stage 3 and you've built your portfolio big enough to support your dream lifestyle, you've made it to Wealth Stage 4. You now have the option not to work and, at the same time, raise your standard of living. You might buy a bigger home, travel more, or just spend more money. You not only have enough compound growth to cover your desired lifestyle, but you also have a little extra to build your portfolio further.

That Reminds Me...

According to official Social Security projections, in 1990 only 4 percent of Americans were over 65. By 2040, the figure will be approximately 25 percent. The number of Social Security beneficiaries will more than double by the year 2040. In 1960, there were 5.1 taxpaying workers to support each Social Security beneficiary. Today, there are 3.3. By 2040, there will be no more than 2, perhaps as few as 1.6. One of four things must happen: We must raise taxes, raise the official Social Security retirement age, radically change the existing Social Security system, or radically change our own personal retirement savings program. The only option we completely control is the last one.

Only about 1 percent of the population make it to Wealth Stage 4. Most people aren't willing to take the time to plan, make the sacrifices, or take the risk. That's right: This stage involves planning, sacrifices, and risk. There's that word risk again! After reading this book, you will understand more about risk and how to manage it properly.

Many of the individuals who make it to this stage are business owners. Their wealth was built from net income, the sale of the business, or both. You can certainly make it to this level without having your own business. This book will show you how.

What's Your Focus Here?

Your two master components are compound growth and risk management. The portfolio is very large, and you might want to focus on reducing volatility. You can do this yourself, but it must be a hobby you enjoy. Most Wealth Stage 4 people hire help in the investment management process. Chapter 9, "How to Find Help," shows you how.

> **Wealth Warning**
>
> Many of the teenagers and 20-year-olds today who are living with their parents in order to save money are actually spending what they save on their image by buying cool clothes and nice cars. This makes them look and feel successful, but they never seem to save enough money to go to college or have their own apartment, much less a home.

Wealth Stage 5

You have accumulated enough assets to produce compound growth well beyond what you would ever spend. You now have the option not to work, raise your standard of living, and bestow large charitable gifts. Once you reach this stage, you need some serious estate-planning help.

If you want to make it to this stage, you could become a famous movie star or corporate executive with a lot of stock options. However, the most common way people make it to this stage is through the sale of a large cash-generating asset such as a business or commercial real estate. You can also get there by building and selling a company. It happens all the time. Just look at the stories in Chapter 1, "Are You Going to Be Rich?"

What's Your Focus Here?

What do you think Wealth Stage 5 people focus on in regard to their money? I can tell you from experience that the answer is risk. The master component is risk and more specifically management of risk. When you make it to this stage, you tend to focus on protection of principal. It doesn't matter whether you make 5 percent or 15 percent on your portfolio. Your needs are covered either way. Therefore, you tend to focus on maintenance instead of compound growth. First, you want to reduce the possibility of a substantial loss. Second, you want to maintain an adequate rate of return.

Certainly, it is great to achieve this stage of wealth, but most people would be content with Stage 3 or 4. Therefore, this material focuses primarily on the first four stages. Making Stage 5 your goal is certainly noble, but it's silly when Stage 4 covers all your needs. Most people who achieve this stage focused on their passion and not necessarily the achievement of this stage of wealth. Following your passion is an important element in the wealth-building process.

How Can You Get There Faster?

You can skip some stages completely if you are starting a business that you believe could substantially increase your income and net worth. This process might get you to Stage 3 or 4 faster. If you take this route, get ready for an exciting ride. There's more risk of failure, and recovery time might be slow depending upon the damage done if the business fails. Therefore, you must be willing to accept failure and keep on going. Before skipping stages and starting your own business, you must be willing to accept the worst thing that can happen. I was willing to accept the risk years ago when I started my own business. I'm glad I did. Would I do it again? You bet I would—even if I couldn't manage money. As long as I had a vision and was excited about it, I would do it. You must be willing to accept big failures and know that you can bounce back in the face of adversity. Remember the story of Abraham Lincoln in Chapter 1.

The Least You Need to Know

- Your idea of wealth should be based upon your desired standard of living, not your neighbor's.
- If you really want to build wealth, don't buy the fancy cars and clothes; keep things simple and live well within your means.
- Take one wealth stage at a time and focus on what's important in each stage.
- In Stage 1, focus on the amount you save and then on the amount of return and risk you want.
- In the later stages, focus on managing the risk in your portfolio.

Chapter 4

How to Become a Saver

In This Chapter

- Developing your Wealth Stage 1 formula
- How to increase your income
- How to decrease expenses
- Calculating how much money you need to consider yourself wealthy
- How to stay on track with your plan

Mark Twain once said, "The secret of getting ahead is getting started. The secret of getting started is breaking your complex overwhelming tasks into small manageable tasks and then starting on the first one." Most people never achieve any significant wealth because they have no idea how to build wealth or even how to get started. There's no class or television show that really shows you how to do it. You might find a few late-night infomercials that sound pretty convincing, but they're really working on their own get-rich agenda to sell you a product. You might find a few books on the subject, but rarely do you find an actual formula that works. If you do find a formula, it is probably either too complicated or too ambiguous. Therefore, I sat down and designed an easy step-by-step formula that would help others get to Wealth Stage 1. It's simple to complete, and it should be your first step in your journey toward wealth. Let's get started.

Wealth Is a Journey, Not a Destination

I've learned that wealth achieved over a long period of time tends to be appreciated more and wealth acquired suddenly tends to be squandered. This is especially evident among lottery winners. An article in the *New York Times* (4/23/95) titled "Ticket to Trouble" stated, "There are no statistics on what happens to jackpot winners. But a growing body of evidence suggests that winning big often brings big, if not ruinous trouble." For example, William Post of Oil City, PA, won a $16.2 million jackpot in 1988. Five years later, he was completely broke, and his brother was in jail charged with hiring a hit man to murder William and his wife for the lottery money.

Treasure Tip

The great wealth hunter Waschka says, "If you always hunt elephants, you may die of starvation. But if you focus on the easier little game like rabbits and birds, you'll be better prepared when the elephant comes along."

Treasure Tip

Looking back at all the wealthy people I've met in my life, it seems that the ones who built their own wealth slowly over time seem to appreciate and maintain it better than those who inherited or married it.

Why do these lottery winners end up in so much trouble? Think about it a minute. They win the lottery, suddenly they feel like they're rich, they begin spending money like never before, and they pay little attention to planning for the future. Who cares about the future when you're rich and you have all this money coming in? That's the problem. These winners see wealth as a destination, and they feel as if they have definitely arrived. What they don't understand is that wealth is a journey, not a destination. You can't get to Wealth Stage 3 and go nuts. You have to continue to be a good steward of your money, which requires some responsibility.

If you want to achieve and maintain wealth throughout your lifetime, you must see wealth as a journey. How most people view wealth is that you hit it big somehow (get rich quick) and then live the good life. If that's your view, stop right now and erase this vision from your mind. Wealth is a way of life. It is a set of beliefs and habits, rather than something material that you attain and then sit back and relax. For example, wealth is born from the initial habit of living within your means. As you saw in Chapter 3, "The Five Stages of Wealth," this journey has many levels and transitions, and most people don't understand them. If you take the time to plan and prepare for each step or transition, you improve your chances of becoming and staying wealthy. It also helps to be patient along the way, especially at the beginning of your journey.

Let's begin your journey by focusing on accomplishing the first level of wealth. Here are the steps to follow:

1. Analyze your current income—and focus on maximizing it.
2. Analyze your current spending habits—and focus on minimizing spending.
3. Estimate how much you need to cover your future expenses (such as your living expenses after retirement) in before-tax dollars.
4. Project the effect of inflation on expenses.
5. Estimate your target portfolio amount (the amount of money you'll need in your portfolio to retire).
6. Estimate your yearly and monthly target savings goal.
7. Achieve your target savings goal.
8. Maintain your plan.

What you are about to embark on is a simple process of estimating income and expenses to find an approximate target savings goal. You could get really serious here with this exercise and build a complex model of expense analysis and wealth projections. If you have a lot of free time on your hands, go for it. I suggest using computer spreadsheets or personal finance software that will do all the calculations for you. To make things easy for now, let's establish some approximate goals so you can at least get started. This chapter walks you, in detail, through each of the steps in the Wealth Builder Worksheet, particularly those steps that require calculations. Read the chapter before using the worksheet, and then make numerous copies of the tearcard in the front of the book so you can update it from year to year to review your progress toward your goals. If you read this chapter before you complete the worksheet, you will understand everything much better.

I've included two examples for you to use. The first is illustrated in the worksheet and the second is illustrated in the text. Both are different and are only there to help you better understand the process.

Wealth Builder Worksheet

1. What is your current yearly income?________________

   Let's say it's $30,000

2. What are your monthly and annual expenses?

   Enter your monthly expenses and multiply by 12:

   ________________ × 12 = ________________

   (Monthly expenses) × 12 = Yearly expenses

   Don't forget to add any additional expenses you see coming in the next year.

   Assuming your monthly expenses are $1,000 a month, that's $12,000 per year.

3. Estimate the income needed to cover your expenses in before-tax dollars.

   Calculate the inverse of your total average tax rate by subtracting your average tax rate from one:

   1.00 –_______ =________________

   1.00 – (Total federal, state, and local income tax rate percentage) = Inverse rate

   If your total tax rate was 28 percent, your inverse would be 72% (1.00 – .28 = .72).

   Convert yearly expenses into a before-tax amount by dividing your yearly expenses by the inverse rate.

   ________________ ÷ ________________ = ________________

   (Total yearly expenses) ÷ (Inverse rate) = Pretax yearly expenses

   Your before tax amount would be $16,666 ($12,000 ÷ .72 = $16,666)

4. Project the effect of inflation on expenses.

   ________________ × ________________ = ________________

   (Pre-tax yearly expenses) × (1.00 + Inflation estimate) = Yearly inflated expenses

Continue this calculation for every year until retirement to get the amount of money you need each year to cover expenses at retirement.

If you assume the inflation rate to be 2 percent, here's what your calculation would look like for the first ten years (rounded to the nearest tenth):

Year 1	$16,666 × 1.02 = 16,999
Year 2	$16,999 × 1.02 = 17,339
Year 3	$17,339 × 1.02 = 17,686
Year 4	$17,686 × 1.02 = 18,040
Year 5	$18,040 × 1.02 = 18,401
Year 6	$18,401 × 1.02 = 18,769
Year 7	$18,769 × 1.02 = 19,144
Year 8	$19,144 × 1.02 = 19,527
Year 9	$19,527 × 1.02 = 19,917
Year 10	$19,917 × 1.02 = 20,315

In ten years, your expenses will be $20,315 assuming an inflation rate of 2 percent. By the way, this is much easier to do on a computer spreadsheet if you have access to one.

5. Estimate your Target Portfolio Goal (TPG).

____________________ ÷ ____________________ =

____

(Yearly inflated expenses) ÷ (Estimated net rate of return) = Target Portfolio Goal

Let's assume you'll retire in ten years (that may not be realistic, but let's use the numbers above), and you'll need $16,127 in income. If you could make a 12 percent rate of return on your portfolio, your target portfolio goal would be (20,315 ÷ .12 = 169,292) $169,292. However, remember that this assumes you'll spend all of your total return on your portfolio. You may want to only spend 75 percent of it so that it keeps growing. If so, use a 9 percent rate of return (.75 × 12 percent).

continues

continued

6. Estimate yearly and monthly TSGs.

   Your yearly TSG is calculated by dividing your TPG by the Future Value Factor, which appears in the future value table in this chapter:

   ______________ ÷ ______________ = ______________

   (Target Portfolio Goal) ÷ (Future Value Factor) = Yearly TSG

   Find your monthly TSG calculation by dividing your yearly TSG by 12:

   ______________________ ÷ 12 = ____________________

   (Yearly TSG) ÷ 12 = Monthly TSG

   Using the 19.6546 factor from the "Future Value of Annuity" chart (see Table 4.4) that corresponds to 12 percent and 10 years, your yearly TSG would be (169,292 ÷ 19.6546 = 8,613) $8,613 and your monthly TSG would be (8,613 ÷ 12 = 717.75) $717.75.

7. Now that you know your TSG, it's time to make it happen.
8. Once you've made it happen and you've achieved Wealth Stage 1, do all you can to maintain your savings amount.

Step 1: Measure and Maximize Your Current Income

Write down on a piece of paper your current yearly salary or income before tax. Under that amount, write this question: What can I do to increase my income now and in the future? Find a peaceful place of solitude and complete 20 answers to this question. If you can't come up with 20 answers, ask a friend to help you. Here are a few ideas to get you started:

- Ask the boss for a raise; prepare a proposal that illustrates what you would do for the raise.
- Offer to take on more responsibility for more pay.
- Start a small income-generating business on the side.
- Consider a second job.

- Present an idea at work that will make the company more profitable.
- Find another job that will pay you what you're worth.

Afterwards, select the best answers and make an effort to implement them. If building wealth is really important to you, you'll take the time to complete this step. As I've mentioned in Chapter 1, "Are You Going to Be Rich?" your journey toward wealth doesn't require a huge salary. However, if you at least attempt to maximize your income, you might shorten the distance you have to travel. There are so many different ways to do this. If you're creative and proactive by nature, you'll have no problem.

The ultimate goal in this step is to calculate the amount of yearly income you want to make before taxes and 401(k) contributions. What amount of income do you need to be happy? Before you answer this question, you might want to complete Step 2 regarding expenses.

> **Treasure Tip**
>
> In 1993, census reports claimed that 205,623 households in the U.S. had incomes of more than $500,000. Of the 2.7 million people making more than $100,000, 89 percent are men, 81 percent are married, 49 percent had postgraduate or professional degrees, and 31 percent had only bachelor's degrees.

Step 2: Measure and Maximize Your Current Expenses

What are your current yearly expenses? How much money do you spend each month? If you're married, how much do both of you spend? The best way to keep track of this is by keeping pen and paper with you for a month. This sounds like a lot of trouble, but remember, we're talking about building your wealth. I always find that whatever is measured seems to improve. If you take the time to do this, you will learn a lot about yourself and quickly see where your money is going. Do this for one month and calculate your actual monthly expenditures. Then, multiply the result by 12. This should give you an approximate idea of your yearly expenses. You could also perform a quick analysis of your checkbook and credit card statements for the last month to get an idea of how most of your money is being spent. You could estimate your cash expenditures by calculating how much cash you've taken out of your account for the month.

> **Treasure Tip**
>
> All work and no play makes Jack a dull boy. Don't forget to record the money you spend for entertainment as a regular expense.

If you prefer a more structured approach, the Weekly Expense Worksheet is designed for you to copy four times, one for each week of the month. (Make five copies if the current month spans five weeks.) You might want to enlarge it to fit a full page. Take a sheet with you and begin recording now. If possible, record every penny you spend for one month. This includes all cash, credit, and checkbook expenditures.

Table 4.1 Weekly Expense Worksheet

Expense Items	Mon	Tues	Wed	Thurs	Fri	Sat	Sun	Total
Auto: Gas								
Auto: Maintenance								
Children: Tuition/ Child Care								
Food: Dining Out/ Credit Card								
Food: Grocery								
Fun:								
Fun:								
Fun: Vacation/ Entertainment								
Home: Furniture								
Home: Housekeeper								
Home: Pest Control								
Home: Rent								
Home: Repair/ Maintenance								
Home: Security Monitoring								
Home: Yard Maintenance								
Insurance: Auto & Liability								
Insurance:								
Insurance: Disability								
Insurance: Health								

Expense Items	Mon	Tues	Wed	Thurs	Fri	Sat	Sun	Total
Insurance: Life								
Loan:								
Loan: Home Mortgage								
Membership: Athletic Club								
Membership:								
Membership Dues:								
Misc:								
Misc:								
Misc: Clothing								
Misc: Contributions/ Gifts								
Misc: Laundry/ Dry Cleaning								
Misc: Medical/ Dental								
Misc: Parking								
Misc: Personal Care								
Misc: Transportation								
Taxes: Property								
Taxes: Income (out of paycheck)								
Taxes: Quarterly Federal								
Taxes: Tax Account to Pay April								
Utility: Electric								
Utility: Gas								
Utility: Phone								
Utility: Water								
Retirement Account (SEP, 401(k))								
Other								
Other								
Other								
Other								

At the end of each week, total each row. Once you have all four sheets, total the corresponding row entries for your weekly total. Do this for four weeks to get a monthly total. For example, total your four weeks' worth of expense for Misc: Personal Care. Using a copy of the Weekly Expense Worksheet, record the sum of the four weekly totals for each expense item to get a full month's total expenses. If you don't want to complete the Weekly Expense Worksheet now, you might want to just estimate your monthly expenses for each category so that you can get started. That's okay, but don't completely disregard the idea of accurately measuring your expenses using the Weekly Expense Worksheet. If you do, you may be basing your entire financial future on incorrect data.

Once you get each monthly total, take a look at where you're spending money. Find the expenses that are unnecessary. What could you do without? Record what you think your expenses should be. This will be your budget. If you want, do the same exercise again next month: Record your actual expenses again and see how close you came. Make this process easy so that it won't seem overwhelming. It's easy to do if you take the time. You might learn more about yourself (and your spouse) than you knew before. This process also may give you more control over your life. I have found that simply by measuring expenses, I tend to be more in control of my spending habits. The goal is to find additional money that you can save.

Using your monthly expense total, calculate a yearly total by multiplying by 12. You need this yearly total for the next step. If you want more exact numbers, look back over the past year's expenses using your checkbook register and credit card statements. You'll want to add yearly expenses such as insurance and property taxes that might not have shown up in your monthly analysis. Set up these numbers on a computer spreadsheet and see what your actual yearly expenses have been. The most effective way to do this is by using one of the personal financial software packages that are available, such as Quicken. This program will help you perform an expense analysis in great detail. For those who don't have a computer, old-fashioned notebook paper works just as well; it just takes longer.

Treasure Tip

So you want to be a doctor or the CEO of a major corporation? The average income for physicians in private practice in 1994 was $218,000. In 1994, the average total compensation of America's 100 highest paid CEOs was $3,554,000, which included bonuses and stock options. This is 190 times the average American worker's income.

You're not finished yet. Do you foresee any change in these spending habits? Some common spending-habit changes occur after marrying, buying a home, having a child, or sending a child to college. Ask yourself what changes you expect to make in the next five years. Estimate the costs and project how much your monthly spending will increase or decrease. Multiply this estimate by 12 to get a yearly figure. The result is the amount of money you will need per year for the added expense, and you should add it into the expense total you've just calculated. Make sure that this result is a conservative figure with some room for error. Pad the amount if you want, just to be sure you've covered all your expenses. Your goal is to establish the lowest amount of expenses you'd be happy to live with now. If you are not satisfied with your current standard of living and you feel you need additional money, then add it. Just remember that if you do so, your target savings goal will be higher and more difficult to achieve.

Step 3: Calculate Your Pretax Income Needs

Step 3 is easy. Estimate your total federal, state, and local income tax rate. You might want to use the income tax rate you calculated in Chapter 2, "Eleven Tools for Building Wealth." Your income tax rate is just a shortcut. If you want to get serious, you could calculate your actual taxes using the current tax tables. You might want to call your CPA if you have one or get a federal and state tax table from the Internal Revenue Service and your state tax agency. Once you have your estimated tax rate, subtract the percentage from 1 to calculate the *inverse* of your tax rate. For example, if your income tax rate is 35 percent, then the equation looks like this:

1 – .35 = .65   .65 is the inverse of your tax rate.

Take your projected yearly expenses that you calculated in the preceding section and divide your expenses by this number. For example, if your estimated yearly expenses add up to $40,000, the equation looks like this:

$40,000 ÷ .65 = $61,538

Therefore, you are going to need $61,538 in income per year before tax in order to maintain your

Words of the Wealthy

The **inverse** of a percentage number is easily calculated by subtracting the number from 1. The inverse of 40 percent is 1 – .4, which is .6 or 60%.

spending habits. In other words, if you had $61,538 in taxable income, you would have approximately $40,000 after you paid your income tax. This may not be an exact figure, but for our purposes here, it's close enough.

> **Words of the Wealthy**
>
> Most people think that **inflation** is the simple rise in prices. The technical definition is an increase in the volume of money and credit relative to available goods, which results in a substantial and continuing rise in the general price level. The rate of inflation is measured by the month-to-month percentage change of the Consumer Price Index (CPI).

Step 4: Consider the Inflation Factor

The next step is to calculate the effect of *inflation* on your expenses in later years. If we continue the example from the last section, we know you need $61,538 each year in today's dollars to cover your expenses, but what about when you retire? What will inflation do to prices by that time?

The only way to answer that question is to make an estimate of future inflation and calculate its effect on your yearly expense needs. This process involves a simple calculation. To calculate the one-year effect of inflation, take the yearly expense total and multiply it by 1 plus your estimate of inflation:

(Yearly expenses before tax) × (1 + estimate of inflation) = Next year's expense estimate

If we use a 3 percent estimate of the annual inflation rate, here is what the calculation looks like:

$61,538 × (1 + .03) = $63,384

This calculation shows you that you will need $63,384 in income next year to cover the same amount of expenses if the inflation rate is 3 percent.

Now that you understand the calculation, you can project further into the future. First, you have to decide how many years you are willing to wait to achieve Stage 3 wealth when your portfolio is producing enough income for you to retire. Let's say you're willing to wait 25 years. Continue the calculation 24 more times. Using the same example, Table 4.2 shows what the result should look like.

Table 4.2 Estimating Future Income Needs Based on Inflation

No. of Years	Year	Pretax Income Needed for Expenses (Base of $61,538)	Estimated Inflation
1	1997	$63,384	3%
2	1998	$65,286	3%
3	1999	$67,244	3%
4	2000	$69,262	3%
5	2001	$71,339	3%
6	2002	$73,480	3%
7	2003	$75,684	3%
8	2004	$77,954	3%
9	2005	$80,293	3%
10	2006	$82,702	3%
11	2007	$85,183	3%
12	2008	$87,738	3%
13	2009	$90,371	3%
14	2010	$93,082	3%
15	2011	$95,874	3%
16	2012	$98,750	3%
17	2013	$101,713	3%
18	2014	$104,764	3%
19	2015	$107,907	3%
20	2016	$111,144	3%
21	2017	$114,479	3%
22	2018	$117,913	3%
23	2019	$121,451	3%
24	2020	$125,094	3%
25	2021	$128,847	3%

As you can see from Table 4.2 in 25 years, you will need approximately $128,847 in income to cover your yearly expense needs. Isn't it scary what inflation of only 3 percent can do to your standard of living? If you have a computer, this calculation is much easier to do on a spreadsheet.

Wealth Warning

Social Security was never intended to fully fund retirement. It's a U.S. Government program established in 1935 for old-age, survivor, and unemployment insurance. It was meant to supplement income, not replace it.

Step 5: Estimate Your Target Portfolio Amount

You have to assume several variables before you can estimate how much money you'll need. You have to estimate your rate of return. Depending upon whom you ask, estimates of rate of return can vary widely. If you ask a conservative investor, the answer could be as low as 5 percent. On the other hand, an aggressive investor might say 15 percent. Your return obviously depends upon the level of risk you take and how your investments perform. The stock market was incredible during the years of 1995 through 1997 when it produced a yearly average return of 28.46 percent. This average is certainly not normal. However, many people new to the market got accustomed to these returns and expected them to continue. This assumption is a grave mistake. Don't get too ambitious with your estimated return factor. For now, let's continue to assume a 10 percent rate of return, which is a little below the average return on the S&P 500 (the major New York Stock Exchange performance index) over the last 40 years.

That Reminds Me...

To achieve real wealth, you must be open minded enough to recognize and break down the self-imposed barriers that keep you in your present financial condition. These barriers are usually mindsets that need a little adjustment. Normally, the adjustment requires a catalyst or disruption to get it started. The most common catalysts and disruptions come from reading and discus-sing ideas with others. Take some time to understand your own barriers about building wealth. Then, discuss them with others who have achieved the level of wealth you desire. How do these people think? How did they overcome their barriers? Did they have similar barriers or different ones? This meeting might be just the catalyst you need.

Divide your yearly before-tax income, adjusted for inflation, by your estimated net rate of return.

$$\frac{\text{Yearly before-tax income adjusted for inflation}}{\text{Estimated net rate of return}} = \text{Target portfolio goal}$$

For example, here is the calculation using the preceding assumptions:

$128,847 ÷ .10 = $1,288,470

Therefore, to retire comfortably and begin living off the return from your portfolio, you'll need a portfolio of assets totaling $1,288,470, producing a rate of return of 10 percent per year.

Isn't this easy? Now, you can measure exactly what you will need in assets to achieve Wealth Stage 3. Don't be overwhelmed by the result. You're about to learn how to build this pool of assets.

Step 6: How to Reach Your Target Portfolio Amount

Using Table 4.2, you can find what your yearly target savings goal should be. Let's review the assumptions before we calculate:

Target portfolio goal	$1,288,470
Yearly before-tax income needed at retirement	$128,847
Estimated rate of return	10 percent
Number of years until retirement	25

In Tables 4.3 through 4.5, find the future value of annuity due factor that corresponds to your assumptions. Look at the top row and find your estimated rate of return of 10 percent. (If you want to use a different rate of return, select it from the table.) Look down the column until you find the factor for the number of years until you retire—in this scenario, 25 years.

Table 4.3 Future Value of Annuity Factors (Annuity Due), Part 1

Years Until You Retire	1%	2%	3%	4%	5%	6%	7%
Rate of Return							
5	5.1520	5.3081	5.4684	5.6330	5.8019	5.9753	6.1533
6	6.2135	6.4343	6.6625	6.8983	7.1420	7.3938	7.6540
7	7.2857	7.5830	7.8923	8.2142	8.5491	8.8975	9.2598
8	8.3685	8.7546	9.1591	9.5828	10.0266	10.4913	10.9780
9	9.4622	9.9497	10.4639	11.0061	11.5779	12.1808	12.8164
10	10.5668	11.1687	11.8078	12.4864	13.2068	13.9716	14.7836
11	11.6825	12.4121	13.1920	14.0258	14.9171	15.8699	16.8885
12	12.8093	13.6803	14.6178	15.6268	16.7130	17.8821	19.1406
13	13.9474	14.9739	16.0863	17.2919	18.5986	20.0151	21.5505
14	15.0969	16.2934	17.5989	19.0236	20.5786	22.2760	24.1290
15	16.2579	17.6393	19.1569	20.8245	22.6575	24.6725	26.8881
16	17.4304	19.0121	20.7616	22.6975	24.8404	27.2129	29.8402
17	18.6147	20.4123	22.4144	24.6454	27.1324	29.9057	32.9990
18	19.8109	21.8406	24.1169	26.6712	29.5390	32.7600	36.3790
19	21.0190	23.2974	25.8704	28.7781	32.0660	35.7856	39.9955
20	22.2392	24.7833	27.6765	30.9692	34.7193	38.9927	43.8652
21	23.4716	26.2990	29.5368	33.2480	37.5052	42.3923	48.0057
22	24.7163	27.8450	31.4529	35.6179	40.4305	45.9958	52.4361
23	25.9735	29.4219	33.4265	38.0826	43.5020	49.8156	57.1767
24	27.2432	31.0303	35.4593	40.6459	46.7271	53.8645	62.2490
25	28.5256	32.6709	37.5530	43.3117	50.1135	58.1564	67.6765
26	29.8209	34.3443	39.7096	46.0842	53.6691	62.7058	73.4838
27	31.1291	36.0512	41.9309	48.9676	57.4026	67.5281	79.6977
28	32.4504	37.7922	44.2189	51.9663	61.3227	72.6398	86.3465
29	33.7849	39.5681	46.5754	55.0849	65.4388	78.0582	93.4608
30	35.1327	41.3794	49.0027	58.3283	69.7608	83.8017	101.0730
35	42.0769	50.9944	62.2759	76.5983	94.8363	118.1209	147.9135
40	49.3752	61.6100	77.6633	98.8265	126.8398	164.0477	213.6096
45	57.0459	73.3306	95.5015	125.8706	167.6852	225.5081	305.7518
50	65.1078	86.2710	116.1808	158.7738	219.8154	307.7561	434.9860

Table 4.4 Future Value of Annuity Factors (Annuity Due), Part 2

Years Until You Retire	8%	9%	10%	11%	12%	13%	14%
Rate of Return							
5	6.3359	6.5233	6.7156	6.9129	7.1152	7.3227	7.5355
6	7.9228	8.2004	8.4872	8.7833	9.0890	9.4047	9.7305
7	9.6366	10.0285	10.4359	10.8594	11.2997	11.7573	12.2328
8	11.4876	12.0210	12.5795	13.1640	13.7757	14.4157	15.0853
9	13.4866	14.1929	14.3974	15.7220	16.5487	17.4197	18.3373
10	15.6455	16.5603	17.5312	18.5614	19.6546	20.8143	22.0445
11	17.9771	19.1407	20.3843	21.7132	23.1331	24.6502	26.2707
12	20.4953	21.9534	23.5227	25.2116	27.0291	28.9847	31.0887
13	23.2149	25.0192	26.9750	29.0949	31.3926	33.8827	36.5811
14	26.1521	28.3609	30.7725	33.4054	36.2797	39.4175	42.8424
15	29.3243	32.0034	34.9497	38.1899	41.7533	45.6717	49.9804
16	32.7502	35.9737	39.5447	43.5008	47.8837	52.7391	58.1176
17	36.4502	40.3013	44.5992	49.3959	54.7497	60.7251	67.3941
18	40.4463	45.0185	50.1591	55.9395	62.4397	69.7494	77.9692
19	44.7620	50.1601	56.2750	63.2028	71.0524	79.9468	90.0249
20	49.4229	55.7645	63.0025	71.2651	80.6987	91.4699	103.7684
21	54.4568	61.8733	70.4027	80.2143	91.5026	104.4910	119.4360
22	59.8933	68.5319	78.5430	90.1479	103.6029	119.2048	137.2970
23	65.7648	75.7898	87.4973	101.1741	117.1552	135.8315	157.6586
24	72.1059	83.7009	97.3471	113.4133	132.3339	154.6196	180.8708
25	78.9544	92.3240	108.1818	126.9988	149.3339	175.8501	207.3327
26	86.3508	101.7231	120.0999	142.0786	168.3740	199.8406	237.4993
27	94.3388	111.9682	133.2099	158.8173	189.6989	226.9499	271.8892
28	102.9659	123.1354	147.6309	177.3972	213.5828	257.5834	311.0937
29	112.2832	135.3075	163.4940	198.0209	240.3327	292.1992	355.7868
30	122.3459	148.5752	180.9434	220.9132	270.2926	331.3151	406.7370
35	186.1021	235.1247	298.1268	379.1644	483.4631	617.7493	790.6729
40	279.7810	368.2919	486.8518	645.8269	859.1424	1145.4858	1529.9086
45	417.4261	573.1860	790.7953	1095.1688	1521.2176	2117.8060	2953.2439
50	619.6718	888.4411	1280.2994	1852.3359	2688.0204	3909.2430	5693.7543

Table 4.5 Future Value of Annuity Factors (Annuity Due), Part 3

Years Until You Retire	15%	16%	17%	18%	19%
Rate of Return					
5	7.7537	7.9775	8.2068	8.4420	8.6830
6	10.0668	10.4139	10.7720	11.1415	11.5227
7	12.7268	13.2401	13.7733	14.3270	14.9020
8	15.7858	16.5185	17.2847	18.0859	18.9234
9	19.3037	20.3215	21.3931	22.5213	23.7089
10	23.3493	24.7329	26.1999	27.7551	29.4035
11	28.0017	29.8502	31.8239	33.9311	36.1802
12	33.3519	35.7862	38.4040	41.2187	44.2445
13	39.5047	42.6720	46.1027	49.8180	53.8409
14	46.5804	50.6595	55.1101	59.9653	65.2607
15	54.7175	59.9250	65.6488	71.9390	78.8502
16	64.0751	70.6730	77.9792	86.0680	95.0218
17	74.8364	83.1407	92.4056	102.7403	114.2659
18	87.2118	97.6032	109.2846	122.4135	137.1664
19	101.4436	114.3739	129.0329	145.6280	164.4180
20	117.8101	133.8405	152.1385	173.0210	196.8474
21	136.6316	156.4150	179.1721	205.3448	235.4385
22	158.2764	182.6014	210.8013	243.4868	281.3618
23	183.1678	212.9776	247.8076	288.4945	336.0105
24	211.7930	248.2140	291.1049	341.6035	401.0425
25	244.7120	289.0883	341.7627	404.2721	478.4306
26	282.5688	336.5024	401.0323	478.2211	570.5224
27	326.1041	391.5028	470.3778	565.4809	680.1116
28	376.1697	455.3032	551.5121	668.4475	810.5228
29	433.7451	529.3117	646.4391	789.9480	965.7122
30	499.9569	615.1616	757.5038	933.3186	1150.3875
35	1013.3757	1300.0270	1668.9945	2143.6489	2753.9143
40	2045.9539	2738.4784	3667.3906	4912.5914	6580.4965
45	4122.8977	5759.7178	8048.7701	11247.2610	15712.0750
50	8300.3737	1210.5353	17654.7170	25739.4510	37503.2500

Your factor for this example should be 108.1818, which we'll call the future value factor. Thus, the calculation to find your yearly TSG looks like this:

Target portfolio goal ÷ Future value factor = Yearly TSG

Here are the actual numbers for the example:

$1,288,470 ÷ 108.1818 = $11,910

To calculate your monthly TSG, divide this number by 12:

$11,910 ÷ 12 = $992.50

Understand that this simple calculation does not consider the effect of taxes on the total return of your investments. If this amount of money were saved in a tax-deferred qualified retirement plan such as a 401(k) or SEP, the math is almost perfect. However, if you are saving in a taxable account (such as a savings account, certificate of deposit, or taxable mutual fund) or the combination of a taxable account and a tax-deferred qualified plan, then you must consider the effect of taxes each year on your total return accumulation.

> **Wealth Warning**
>
> This process of finding your target savings goal is not difficult to complete, but it is easy to make a mistake. Once you complete all the necessary steps and calculations, be sure to go back and check your math.

Let's assume your net tax liability on dividends, interest, and capital gains is 30 percent. If you make an average total return of 10 percent, then you could subtract 30 percent of the 10 percent return to get a net total return of 7 percent. This 7 percent can then be used to estimate your target portfolio return. (That is, you should choose a 7 percent rate of return factor from Table 4.2 rather than the 10 percent rate of return factor from Table 4.3 before making your calculation.) However, remember this is still only an estimate. Your capital gains may not all accrue each year, which means that there will be irregular capital gains taxes to pay each year, depending upon when your investment transactions result in a capital gain.

Step 7: Strategies for Achieving Your Target Savings Goal

Treasure Tip

Many wealthy people I know built part of their fortune using residual income, which is income derived over time from previous efforts or past accomplishments that continue to produce cash flow. This includes rental income and income from books, tapes, or other media that continue to sell with little additional effort.

If you are overwhelmed by your target portfolio size, don't be concerned. Don't forget that this amount is based upon some assumptions you made that can be adjusted. First, you could decrease the assumed inflation rate used to project your future living expenses. Second, you could accept some more risk and increase your estimated total return assumption. Third, you could extend the number of years you are willing to wait before you reach Wealth Stage 3. Fourth, when you retire, you could move to some developing country and live on less money!

If you want to achieve your target savings goal, you have to ask yourself what factors you have the most control over. You have the least control over things like inflation and total return. You have the most control over expenses and the amount of money you save. You have some control over income, but reducing your expenses is usually easier than increasing income. It may not be as glamorous, but it is effective in achieving a larger savings goal. The less you spend, the more you have available for savings. The following list of ideas is designed to reduce your expenses.

- **Lower expenses.** Find expenses you can do without. Don't eat out as much. Turn down your heat or air conditioning at night or when you're gone. Use the phone book instead of information when you can. Stop smoking and you'll not only save the money you spend on cigarettes, you'll also save on your health insurance, not to mention medical bills later.
- **Avoid buying lottery tickets.** If you understand the odds of winning the lottery, you will never buy a ticket.
- **Home and auto maintenance actually lower expenses.** I just replaced my 15-year-old air-conditioning system with a new one. My electric bills are less, and my home is much cooler when it's hot outside.

- **Don't use life insurance for investment purposes.** This is one of the most common mistakes investors make. The cost of the insurance and commissions drain your investment, which decreases the total return you get. A friend who is an insurance agent says, "But the investment grows tax deferred." My reply is, "I don't care! It costs too much, and the policy holder is limited to only a handful of investment choices that usually are mediocre at best." My suggestion is to separate your investment money from your life insurance. Consider a less expensive term policy and depositing the savings in a no-load mutual fund.

  Warning: Do not drop your existing life insurance first. If you plan to change to the term policy, do it first. Once it is set up, then cancel your past insurance. You don't want to be uncovered. If you can't get a term policy because of a preexisting condition, you will have your existing policy to fall back on.

- **Shop by phone for life insurance.** You can get quality life insurance by phone. Here are three companies that will shop the term life insurance market for you and show you the best deal:

Select Quote	800-343-1985
Quotesmith	800-431-1147
Master Quote	800-337-5433

  These companies will contract with a medical technician who will come to your office to draw blood and fill out medical forms.

- **Save money when you travel.** Smart travelers know that airlines want to charge business travelers more money than vacationers. They assume that business travelers can write off the travel and therefore are more willing to pay higher prices. By simply staying at your destination over a Saturday night, you can sometimes save 75 percent on your airline ticket. You can also book hotel rooms cheaper in large cities by using services that offer more inexpensive lodging by purchasing rooms in bulk. Here are a few companies that offer this service:

Hotel Reservations	800-964-6835
Express Reservations	800-356-1123
Quickbook	800-789-9887

- **Consider increasing your insurance deductible.** If you increase your deductible, your insurance premiums should drop considerably. Insurance was designed to protect you from big, catastrophic losses. However, many people today have their windshields replaced with insurance money. A broken windshield is far from a catastrophic loss. People who make insurance claims on such items don't realize they are actually paying more for the windshield in the long run than they would if they had a larger deductible. Call your agent and ask him or her how much you would save by boosting your deductible.

Step 8: Stay on Track

The last step is to maintain your plan. Each year, you should redo all the calculations for the Wealth Builder Worksheet and the Weekly Expense Worksheet in this chapter. You should measure your monthly expenses each month, if not quarterly. If you continue to measure your expenses, you will be better able to meet your goal. I guarantee that your plan will change over time. Some of the changes will be small and some will be large. Your success in maintaining your plan depends a great deal upon several things:

> **Wealth Warning**
>
> Associate with other people who share your ambitions and aspirations and who are willing to share ideas and support you in your efforts. Look for win/win relationships. Avoid those people who pull you down and drain your enthusiasm.

- **Your flexibility and creativity.** You must be willing to respond to the inevitable changes that life brings. You must be able to handle adversity.
- **Your organizational skills.** You must keep current, at least yearly, with all the elements of your plan.
- **Your willingness to work on your plan.** Your journey toward wealth will take some time, so make certain you enjoy the journey; the payoff will be worth it.

The Least You Need to Know

- Wealth is a way of life—a set of beliefs and a mixture of habits that begin by living within your means.
- To live within your means, you must be willing to measure your spending habits occasionally in order to understand your means and maximize your savings capacity.
- Don't forget to consider taxes and inflation when doing any future wealth planning.
- Along your journey, focus on what you have the most control over, which is the amount of money you spend and the amount of money you save.

Chapter 5

The Secrets of Millionaires

In This Chapter

- Saving money systematically each month
- How you can make money shopping
- The characteristics of very wealthy people
- Why passion is key to the wealth-building process
- Avoiding debt and paying cash

I realized long ago that if you want to achieve anything great in life, find the people who are already the best at what you want to do and imitate them. First, identify their habits. What are they doing on a consistent basis that enables them to achieve their results? Second, what are the key characteristics that enable them to achieve their results? This is what I've done for more than 13 years in business and for more than 30 years in my life. I am fascinated by what enables some people to build great wealth and why others never seem to get there no matter how hard they try.

Remember the couple I mentioned in Chapter 1, "Are You Going to Be Rich?" Mr. and Mrs. Post, who never made more than $30,000 per year, yet their portfolio was worth more than $800,000? Not to mention the $240,000 in homes they had paid cash for as gifts for their two daughters and the fully funded $100,000 college education account! How could this couple have so much money with so little income? Well, that is exactly what I asked, and they said, "We saved it and invested it in no-load funds." I said, "Please tell me your story. There's got to be more to this, right?" They sat back and shared some simple truths that every investor should follow. I call them the seven habits of very wealthy people, and I detail them in this chapter.

The Seven Habits of Very Wealthy People

The seven habits for building wealth include saving every month, staying out of debt, shopping before you buy, buying used when you can, taking care of your stuff, investing in stocks, and taking time to plan your future.

1. Be a Consistent Saver

The Posts said that each month, no matter what they made in salary, they put money in savings and invested in no-load mutual funds. They said, "No matter what happens, pay yourself first and make it a habit." The combination of systematic savings and compound growth is incredible. Here are several ways you can start saving money now:

- **Maximize your 401(k) or SEP-IRA contributions.** This is the easiest thing to do because the deposits are usually automatically deducted from your paycheck, and you only make an investment decision once in a while. If your company or employer offers one of these plans, take advantage of it now and maximize your contributions. Millionaires are made of these plans. The assets grow tax deferred, and you get the benefit of using Uncle Sam's money in the compounding process.
- **If you are self-employed, consider starting your own SEP-IRA (an IRA plan for self-employed people).** You'll be able to shelter up to 15 percent of your income until you retire. This powerful step is simple to implement. All you have to do is fill out an application, make a deposit, and you're on your way.
- **Maximize your IRA or Roth IRA contribution.** An IRA is an Individual Retirement Account into which you can deposit a maximum of $2,000 of earned income each year. The true benefit of the IRA is that all interest, dividends, and capital gains are tax deferred until they are withdrawn. The second benefit is the flexibility of investment alternatives that are available. You can invest in CDs, stocks, bonds, and mutual funds. Because there are more than 5,000 different mutual funds, your alternatives are almost endless. The third benefit is convenience. An IRA is simple to start. All you

have to do is fill out an application and make a deposit. The regular IRA is deductible from your income, which lessens your tax burden. You can withdraw money from this IRA after you are 59 1/2 years old, but it's taxable as ordinary income. The Roth IRA is different because it's not deductible from your income, but it can be withdrawn after you are 59 1/2 years old tax-free. The power of the IRA is in the compounding, not the deduction from your taxes. Just because you can't deduct the Roth IRA doesn't mean it's not attractive.

The tax deductibility of your deposit depends upon your income and involvement in a qualified plan. If you are not enrolled in a qualified retirement plan, you may be able to deduct your deposit from your total taxable income. Be sure to check with the IRS, your CPA, or a financial planner to find out more about your situation.

- **Write yourself a check.** Before you start paying your bills each week or each payday, write yourself a check and deposit the check in a separate account. The whole idea is to pay yourself before anyone else. Your 401(k) works the same way; it comes out of the check before you get it. Your goal should be to save your target savings goal and then use the remainder to budget your spending. Act as if the target savings goal amount doesn't even exist and budget accordingly.
- **Let a mutual fund direct-debit your account.** Most mutual funds offer a direct-debit feature that automatically withdraws a predetermined amount from your checking account each month. This is one of the easiest ways to save money. Each month at bill-paying time, just record the withdrawal in your check register. Don't be afraid of this feature. Try it for a year and cancel if you don't like it.
- **Save your pennies, nickels, dimes, and quarters.** I spend only whole dollar bills and save my change every day in a bowl. When the bowl is full, I deposit it in

Treasure Tip

If you can't deduct your IRA deposit, you might want to make a Roth IRA deposit anyway. The assets grow tax deferred (you don't pay tax on any interest or other income), and you get to make tax-free withdrawals. With the freedom to invest in almost any liquid security, the Roth IRA is a powerful tool.

my investment account. The bank's not too excited about counting all those coins, but they get over it!

- **Save your raises.** Another trick is to ignore any raises in income when budgeting for expenses. When you get a raise, save the entire raise. Instead of increasing your spending habits, increase your saving habits. Let the raise boost your saving percentage.

I can't guarantee you'll be rich if you use all these strategies, but I can promise you that they certainly increase your chances.

2. Pay Cash When You Can

Debt is a tool, and it works just like a lever. The word *leverage* is often used when people refer to debt, and that's exactly how debt can operate. The more debt you have, the more buying power you control. However, many people in today's world have gone crazy with debt, and the result is a record number of bankruptcies. Debt is okay if you know how to use it. I have few simple rules that I live by when it comes to debt. It's okay to leverage your home, and it's okay to leverage a business venture as long as you can afford to cover the payments. However, it's not okay to leverage your self-image. Using debt to live in a lifestyle you can't afford is wrong.

Many rich individuals pay cash for everything and avoid debt (except for their home mortgage). Instead of borrowing money to purchase an item, they wait until they save enough money to buy the item with cash. Save money for the things you want and pay cash.

Here are four ideas that will help you eliminate debt:

1. **Refinance your mortgage.** Shop around when mortgage rates drop to see if you can get a better fixed rate. If you plan to stay in your home for more than two years, and if you can improve your mortgage rate by as much as 2 percent, you should consider refinancing. This may reduce your mortgage payments and reduce the amount of money you spend each year on interest payments. Reduce or avoid points and origination fees. These are often negotiable. Offer to refinance if the mortgage company will reduce their fees.
2. **Use only low-interest credit cards.** Do some research to find the credit card with the lowest possible rate. You must understand the tactics of credit card companies. Don't be fooled by the introductory rate they tease you with in order to get you as a cardholder. Ask the company whether the rate they quote is an introductory

rate. Also, you might want to consider getting a debit card. These cards look like a standard credit card but directly debit your checking account for purchases. Because you are not financing your purchase, there is no finance charge. Check your local bank for this option.

> **Treasure Tip**
>
> Debt used to build a business or increase cash flow is acceptable. Consumer and credit card debt used to build your image in society is not acceptable and will reverse the wealth-building process.

3. **Home equity loans can help.** If you have a great deal of credit card debt and you own your own home, you might consider applying for a home equity loan and using the loan money to pay off your credit card debt. Avoid origination fees and points, which tend to counteract your overall interest savings. Check with your tax preparer to find out whether this interest is deductible. Getting a home equity loan to pay another debt is one way to convert a non–tax-deductible expense to a tax-deductible one. If you have any equity in your home and you anticipate having to borrow money to buy a car, consider a home equity loan. You'll more than likely get a lower interest rate and, at the same time, you'll be able to deduct the interest on the loan from your taxable income. BE SURE THAT YOU DON'T BORROW MORE MONEY THAN YOUR HOME IS WORTH! There are commercials on TV telling you that you can borrow up to 125 percent of your home's value. This is an easy way to get into trouble.
4. **Pay more each month on your mortgage.** If you can afford to add money to your mortgage payment each month, you will reduce the overall interest costs on your mortgage and speed up the time it takes to retire your mortgage. If you can double your payments, your home will

> **Treasure Tip**
>
> Don't be seduced by the low introductory rates on credit cards. If you read the fine print on most of these cards, you'll see that much higher rates kick in after the first year.

be paid off more quickly. You might also want to consider a 15-year mortgage versus the typical 30-year mortgage. You'll pay a little more each month, but you'll save an enormous amount of money in interest later. Be sure to check with your mortgage holder about how your extra payments can apply to your loan.

3. Shopping Saves You Money

Our society today is known for its impatience. Our attitude has become, "We want it right now, and we get what we want!" This attitude doesn't help motivate anyone to shop. I'm not talking about going shopping. I'm talking about doing your homework before you buy anything of significance.

The Posts also said that they shopped extensively before they bought anything. This is a simple concept, but few people take the time. It is my belief that women by nature are shoppers and men are not. My personal habit is to get into the store, buy exactly what I need, and get out of there. I've learned my lesson. Now I ask everyone I know where I can get the best price. This saves me a great deal of time. If you hate to shop, get some help from others who enjoy it. Take a moment and think about your own habits. Do you take the time to shop around? Are you an impulsive buyer?

- **Shop at warehouse clubs.** I learned many years ago that I could save a lot of money by shopping at warehouse clubs. It was difficult to store the large quantities when I lived in my tiny, 500-square-foot apartment, but it is much easier now in my house. As you can imagine, I spend a lot of money at Sam's Club.
- **Buy seasonal items out of season.** When you do shop, think opposite of the crowd's thinking. When do most people buy the item you want? If you want to buy a boat, start shopping at the end of the summer. Owners will accept a lower price, knowing the expense of keeping it another winter in storage. Most people buy their boats in the early spring. Avoid the buying pressure, and get it cheap later in the summer. You can say the same thing about lawn mowers, convertible automobiles, and landscaping materials. If snow is a problem in the winter, buy a snow blower in the late spring. If you time your purchases right and negotiate properly, you might pay only a fraction of the normal in-season price. Many times, I put off buying an item just so I can wait until the off season to buy it cheaper. Have you ever been to the Disney World in

Orlando during the month of September? It's great! All the kids are back in school, and the place isn't crowded. I've also been there between Christmas and New Years...big mistake!

- **Learn to haggle.** The United States is the only country I know where people accept paying the full price on merchandise without negotiation. I'm guilty of this, too. However, I've learned to always ask, "Is there any way I can get a better price on this?" And it works. Contrary to popular belief, this is not rude. A few months ago, I offered to purchase $8,000 worth of antiques from a large antique warehouse. I asked whether it would give me a discount for the amount of money I wanted to spend. They gave me more than 10 percent off, which added up to $800. What a great reward for asking such an easy question. The next time you buy a big-ticket item, negotiate.
- **Delay purchases of items you don't need.** Before you rush out to the store or pick up the telephone to buy that widget you just have to have, write it down, and think about it for a week. Then, ask yourself whether you still want it as much. How many things do you have in your closet, storage room, or drawers that you used only a few times? I've practiced this tactic over the past five years and even built a file of things I've wanted to buy. Would you believe that I've bought only maybe 10 percent of them? This habit really cuts down on the amount of stuff you'll be selling in your next garage sale. Remember that the more stuff you have, the more responsibility you take on.

Don't confuse shopping with buying. My associate Linda shared this story with me: "One of the ongoing jokes in our family is about the time when my sister-and-law and I went shopping and found a huge sale. She returned from the store with her car full of bags. As she went through each bag, she kept referring to the sale prices and how much money she had saved. My brother, who was about to bust a blood vessel, wasn't too happy about all the money she had saved. I don't know if it was just coincidence,

Words of the Wealthy

The word **haggle** comes from the Old English term *heawan,* which means to beat or cut. Haggling is the process of negotiating the lowest price possible in a purchase transaction. The U.S. is one of the few countries where haggling is not a normal part of everyday shopping.

but they got divorced a short time later. Anyway, any time we find a sale, we show it to the family with the introduction of 'Look how much money I saved!'" The moral of this story is that just because it's a good price doesn't mean you are saving money if you're buying something you don't need.

4. Consider Previously Owned Merchandise

The Posts often bought previously owned merchandise, especially if they could find good quality at lower prices. They spent a lot of time shopping for used items in the local want ads. They said they saved a lot of money over the years by focusing on used instead of new cars. They bought quality used cars from previous owners and eliminated the commission paid to the salesperson, along with the heavy depreciation incurred in the first year. Don't be a fanatic about buying everything new. Consider a used car before you purchase a new one. Consider antique furniture instead of new. Check the want ads before you buy. Sometimes I use last week's ads, because if the seller still has the item, he is usually more motivated to sell it at a cheaper price.

Used cars seem more attractive than ever before. New car prices have risen approximately 29 percent since 1990, and consequently, buyers are not as eager to buy more. We have also seen a huge supply of program cars or previously leased cars hit the market. This large supply of two- and three-year old cars has resulted in more competitive prices.

Treasure Tip

If possible, sell your own car instead of trading it in. You have a better chance of getting a higher price than a dealer will offer you on trade.

If you have to buy a new car, call eight of the surrounding dealers within four hours driving distance and ask for the best price on the automobile of your choice. Be sure to be specific with your model and desired options.

I tried to buy a used Chevy Suburban two years ago but could not find one available at a reasonable price. They were in such high demand that the used prices actually exceeded the new prices. Therefore, I had to look at new models. I did some homework and found a company in California called IntelliChoice (800-227-2665) that offers a service called Just the Facts, which gives you dealer's cost and discounts available on most cars available here in the U.S. The service is $14.95 by mail and $17.99 by fax. I called IntelliChoice to find the dealer's cost on the model I wanted. I then called eight dealers around the state and actually negotiated a price $200 above the dealer's cost. If you have to buy new, IntelliChoice can help you.

When you buy a used automobile, focus on quality and resale value. In the mid 1980s, I purchased a used, one-year-old Jeep Cherokee with no frills or extras. I paid $7,000 for it, drove it 20,000 miles, and sold it 18 months later for $6,800.

Wealth Warning

Before you buy a used car, take it to an independent car repair service for a check-up. If you unknowingly buy a poor-quality, unreliable car, you may end up with big problems later. There's nothing worse than sinking your hard-earned money into something that's not reliable—except having to sell it later.

If you want to know approximately what an automobile is worth, call your bank and ask for blue book values. There are three prices to notice. First is the loan value, which is the amount of money a bank is willing to loan a customer to buy the car. Second is the trade-in value or wholesale price, which is what a car dealer might be willing to pay for the car on a trade. Third is the retail price, which you might pay if you were buying it from a used car dealer. Your goal as a buyer is to buy the car at or below the loan value. Your goal as a seller is to sell it at or above retail. Either way, if you don't get the price you want, you have to be willing to walk away.

If you do get a loan to buy a car, be sure to shop several banks for the best rate. If you do this before you look for a car, you'll be better prepared to negotiate.

That Reminds Me...

If at all possible, don't lease a car. The commission and financing charges are all disguised in the payment, which makes it difficult to make an intelligent decision. Most of the time, the lease is much more expensive in the long run. If you purchase a used vehicle, take care of it with regular maintenance, and sell it later, your total out-of-pocket expense should be much less than the cost of a lease agreement.

Consider antique furniture. A few years ago, a dear friend taught me an invaluable lesson. I was looking for furniture for my office, and he said, "Larry, don't waste your money on new furniture. Buy functional antiques." He explained that, "You can depreciate them on your balance sheet as they appreciate in value." This man is a genius. My office is full of these antiques. Not only are they beautiful, but they have also appreciated since I bought them. You can certainly find some good deals at local antique stores, but the best deals happen at estate auctions where you can cut out the middleman. Where do you think the antique stores get their inventory?

Don't misunderstand my point about buying used merchandise. You should focus on quality. Whether you buy new or used, you must focus on quality and resale value. Always research the big-ticket items in the classified ads before you buy, and look at how they fall in price relative to their original retail price. How do they fall in price each year? Are there any consumer reports out on the product? Go to the library and look in the periodical index for the particular item you want to buy. See whether any studies exist. *Consumer Reports* is a magazine that can save you a lot of money. It does studies on different products regarding quality, maintenance, and resale value. Why not subscribe?

5. Be a Great Steward

Another pearl of wisdom the Posts shared with me involved stewardship, which in their case was simple maintenance. They said they took care of what they owned. They said that it is amazing how long things will last if you take good care of them. They bought great quality items and took great care of them. For example, I have a tree farm, and I needed a tractor. I bought a John Deere because of its track record of holding its resale value and the local service dealer's dedication to servicing the tractor after the sale. I bought a top-quality machine and paid a lot of money for it, but the dealership actually helps me be a great steward.

More than likely, the largest "machine" you have is your automobile. If you want it to last a long time and hold its resale value, you must conduct regular maintenance. The Posts had both of their automobiles serviced every 4,000 miles, which included an oil and filter change. They also waxed their cars every six months. These simple steps helped keep their cars running better and helped maintain the resale value.

Home maintenance is also important. Have your heating and air-conditioning system checked once a year to prolong the life of your equipment. Pay for a good pest control service now so you don't have to pay later for termite damage. Prevent exterior damage of your home by regularly cleaning out your gutters and replacing the old ones. If you have to, get someone to help you.

6. Learn the Basics of Investing

The next habit this couple taught me was to develop a basic understanding of the stock and bond markets. They studied the basics, knew the benefit of owning *stocks*, invested in stocks through no-load funds, and learned on their own the hard way. They learned a great deal from the mistakes they made and understood that investing money in the stock market involves occasionally making mistakes. In spite of all that, they kept learning more each day and stayed the course.

If you feel uncomfortable with your investment knowledge, get proactive and do something about it now. There is no excuse for ignorance. Books and classes available can teach you everything you need to know.

Words of the Wealthy

When you buy shares of **stock** directly or through a mutual fund, you become part owner of a company. These shares can build your wealth by paying you dividends and by rising in price.

The best way to learn is to start investing. You'll want to learn because your money is at stake. The next best way to learn is to join an organization dedicated to educating investors. One of the best organizations I've found is the American Association of Individual Investors (800-428-2244). Call and ask for an information packet. You might also read some books on stock investing. Here are some of my favorites:

Beating the Street, Peter Lynch, retired manager of Fidelity Magellan

One Up on Wall Street, Peter Lynch

Value Investing, Ben Graham (This may get a little technical, but Ben is the father of value investing.)

Bogle on Funds, John Bogle, the past chairman of Vanguard Funds

That Reminds Me...

When you purchase a bond or mutual fund, you are essentially buying IOUs of companies or the government. The total interest paid each year is your reward for loaning the money. Additional reward comes when interest rates fall and the price of the bond increases. The reverse is also true. If rates go up, the price of the bond will fall. A bond is simply a source of future cash flow that can be bought and sold at different prices until maturity. However, at the bond's maturity, the bondholder is paid only the face amount or maturity value of the bond along with the appropriate interest amount.

7. Do Your Homework

Finally, Mr. and Mrs. Post also did their homework. They took time to research their options before they made an investment, and they understood that quick decisions get you hurt in the market. Rumors get started and before you know it, a "hot tip" turns out to be a cold nightmare. They recognized and avoided the traps.

Treasure Tip

Time is money and requires just as much management as your money. If you don't have a day planner, get one. If you do have one, shop around and make sure yours is the best for your needs. I've used a day planner since I was 13 years old. They just make my life so much easier.

Don't forget to measure the results of your portfolio. Not measuring results is one of the most common mistakes made by individual investors. They invest for years, never actually knowing their portfolio's true performance on a monthly or yearly basis. They might estimate it, but they rarely do it accurately, and they almost never compare it to the proper benchmark indexes.

Each year, you should reevaluate your progress toward your wealth goal. Do the calculations in Chapter 4, "How to Become a Saver," again if you need to. This will help you stay on track. Did you know that planes that fly on autopilot from the U.S. to Hawaii are off track almost 95 percent of the time? It's because of wind. The autopilot resets the plane's course every few minutes because the wind keeps knocking it off course. The plane makes it because the autopilot mechanism continues to repeatedly reset the compass bearing. Your journey toward wealth is similar. You'll experience wind along the way that will blow you off course. Don't forget to reset your compass bearing at least once a year.

Do You Have What It Takes to Be Wealthy?

What does it take to be wealthy? Is there a trick? If you want to improve your odds of achieving your desired level of wealth, you have to think like a wealthy person. Over the last 10 years in the investment business, I have spoken to thousands of wealthy individuals like Mr. and Mrs. Post. I've learned a great deal from these people. Mr. and Mrs. Post taught me the seven habits in this chapter, but they and other wealthy individuals also taught me things that went unspoken. These unspoken lessons were characteristics they portrayed. Most of these people were happy and enthusiastic about life, and I have a lot of admiration for them. I tried to avoid the people who were consistently unhappy. I had so much admiration for the ones with great attitudes about life that I began to make notes about them. It was fascinating because they all seem to have several mental characteristics in common. The rest of this section presents the four most common characteristics.

Treasure Tip

According to the Census Bureau, the number of poor people making less than the poverty threshold of $15,000 per year in the U.S. fell by more than 1 million in 1993—the first decline in five years.

Follow Your Passion

Most of my friends know me and the amount of passion I have for life. I do what I love to do, and somehow little miracles happen almost every day. I have come to realize that the more I focus on my dreams and passions, the more I get accomplished. When you focus on your dreams and passions, you live from your soul. Unfortunately, not many people do this. Most of those who do understand the power in this. When you live from your soul, you become like a magnet, drawing everything you need into your life that will help you accomplish your goal. That might sound like a little hocus-pocus, but I speak from experience.

The great irony today in society is that most people are really afraid of following their dreams. If people would let themselves focus on what they are passionate about in life, they not only would live a happier life, but they would also be able to accomplish more. They would naturally be more competitive. They would achieve greater accomplishments than they thought possible.

The world is so competitive now that markets around the world have opened up their doors to outside consumers. To compete in any business today, you have to work harder and be smarter than your competition. In the long run, the winners in any industry will be those companies and individuals who were passionate enough about their work to spend the time and effort it takes to produce outstanding products and services. Without this passion, a company or individual will be less likely to make the effort or spend all night to meet a deadline. During the first four years of building my company, I spent at least one full night a month in my office working. Sometimes I would work 32 hours straight. I've fallen asleep right in the middle of a conversation with a client.

It's not that I'm an advocate of working this many hours. (It's unhealthy.) My point is that I was excited enough about my company to want to. The question I'm asking here is this: In your present position, are you willing to work all night on a project if you have to? If the answer is no, then you need to seriously consider making a job change or starting your own business doing what you enjoy.

The happiest wealthy people I know have a passion for what they do, which seems to naturally create a certain level of tenacity and perseverance toward achieving their goals. They have a vision, and they are enthusiastic about life. Their enthusiasm is sincere, and it comes from deep inside. They don't necessarily have a passion for building wealth. Wealth, for them, is a result of their passion and effort for the work they do.

A student asked me recently, "If you could change anything in the business world, what would it be?" I told her that if everyone loved what he were doing in his life today, or if everyone at least had a plan to achieve this, the world would be a better place. There would be less frustration, anger, and unhappiness. People would feel more gratification.

When you love what you do, your chances of great achievement improve dramatically. If you are unsure about where your passion lies, the following five questions will give you some ideas to consider. These questions could change your life for the better. It all depends upon how honest you are with yourself when you answer each question. There are no right or wrong answers, so relax and enjoy yourself. Write down exactly what comes to mind. Do not judge any answer! Let your mind go and list anything that comes to mind, no matter how impossible it might seem. Write each question at the top of a separate page, go to a quiet place where you will not be interrupted, and spend some quality time with yourself answering these questions:

> **Treasure Tip**
>
> "Great dancers are not great because of their technique; they are great because of their passion."
>
> —Martha Graham

1. Your doctor calls and tells you that in exactly six months, you will die a peaceful death due to a weird, unknown virus. What would you do during this six-month period? Whom would you spend time with? What activities would you spend time doing? What would be important to you? (List at least 20 answers.)
2. An unknown relative dies and leaves you a portfolio of cash totaling $2,000,000. What would you do? Whom would you spend time with? What activities would you spend time doing? What would be important to you? Would you quit work? How would you spend your money? (List at least 20 answers.)
3. What three great endeavors would you dare to attempt if you were guaranteed you could not fail?
4. What do you want more of in your life? (List at least 20 answers.)
5. What do you want less of in your life? (List at least 20 answers.)

The answers to these questions give you insight into your most important values in life. They illustrate what's really important to you and, in the case of number 5, what you want less of in your life. They should act as a guide in your search for what you really want in life. Use these answers not only to find your passion, but also use them as parameters against which you compare any major endeavor in life.

If you really take the time to list 20 or more answers, you might find some things you enjoy doing that you haven't participated in for a long time. One of your answers could be something you're passionate about that you can use as a business idea. It might be another position within a company or your own company.

If you can't figure it out now, put the pages away and try this exercise again in a week. Be sure to change your surroundings next time. Sit in a comfortable spot with no interruptions. Try it a third time if you have to.

Be a Decision Maker

> **Wealth Warning**
>
> Remember that no matter what you do in life, you will always reap what you sow. In your journey toward wealth, make sure your work helps others or improves the world in some way. If not, your efforts will eventually backfire and reverse the wealth-building process.

The wealthiest people I know are good decision makers. They don't procrastinate or live in denial. They take the time to identify all the issues, research the alternatives, and select the best answer. They don't waste too much time worrying about things they have little control over. They also look carefully at all the possible consequences of each decision. They list the pros and cons, take time to think about all the options, and finally ask themselves, "What is the worst thing that can happen?" If they can accept the worst possible outcome, they press forward. If not, they hold back. They understand zero-based thinking.

Develop Discipline

Discipline is simply sticking to a decision. If you make decisions based on your passions, the discipline should come naturally. The clients I have who built their wealth from the ground up have a certain discipline that helps them adhere to the simple habits necessary to build wealth. Climbing the social ladder is unimportant to them. They focus instead on what they are passionate about.

Discipline is simply a subconscious habit that is established by repetition. It's difficult to start a habit, but I'm told that after 21 days, it becomes part of your life. Here's an idea. For 21 days, take 15 minutes in the afternoon to plan tomorrow. This will give your brain time to think about what you have to do, which will help you get closer to your vision.

Be Patient

Wealthy people are patient and maintain a long-term outlook. They plan for the future and do what it takes to build wealth, and over time, they naturally know they will succeed. When they're faced with failure, they get right back on track again and go for it. They understand that wealth building is a journey, not a destination. It's a practice of patient habits that naturally produces riches.

Have Faith

Having faith may be the most powerful tool in this book. All great accomplishments require faith. I'm talking about faith in yourself, faith in your dreams, faith in others, and spiritual faith. You must have faith in yourself and your abilities. The wealthy people I know look at life with an open mind. What they don't know or understand, they do what it takes to learn. Faith in yourself is something that can be learned. Numerous material, classes, and counselors can help you develop more faith in yourself.

> **Treasure Tip**
>
> Along with faith in yourself, faith in others is almost as important. One of the most common characteristics among wealthy people is their belief in the inherent good in others. I don't know how I could have achieved anything significant in my life without my belief and faith in the people who helped me.

Most wealthy people I know also have a strong spiritual faith. Regardless of your beliefs or religion, it is difficult to imagine that we are not all connected in some way. All that you do in life affects the world in some little way. Like the ripples from a rain drop in a pool of water, what you do in life has some effect on the world. You matter, and your life is important. If everyone lived his or her life with this belief, the world would have much more faith to work with. My hope is that this material, in some way, gives you faith and that you are able to make a greater difference in this world.

Be Willing to Sacrifice

Every great accomplishment involves a sacrifice. To achieve any great endeavor, you must first decide exactly what you want. Then, you must be willing to make the sacrifices necessary. You can only focus on one thing at a time, and that means that you have to sacrifice your focus on other endeavors. If you have several passions in life, you know how difficult it is to choose one passion to focus on. I have several passions in life, and it's not easy making the sacrifices. I've learned that the bigger the endeavor, the bigger the sacrifices. Most people aren't willing to make the sacrifices. Don't be like most people!

The Least You Need to Know

- The basis of all the habits of wealthy people involves maximizing income, minimizing expenses, and making your savings work for you.
- If you want to achieve anything great in life, find the people who are already the best at what you want to do and imitate them.
- If you will delay most major purchases by writing them down, filing them away, and not thinking about them for a month or more, you may save a lot of money and prevent a lot of mistakes.
- Buying used cars and antique furniture can save you a fortune in commission and depreciation expenses.
- To be really wealthy in life, you must have enough passion for what you do that you lose yourself in your work.
- Building wealth requires certain habits that are easy to implement and maintain.

Think Like a Leader

by Andrew J. Dubin

Gary, the vice president of operations, was walking in the company parking lot when he encountered Rachel, an industrial engineer who was one of the newly appointed production supervisors. The vice president and the supervisor then walked together toward the same building. While they were walking, the supervisor said, "Hmmm, we must have morale problems. Look at all the litter and soft-drink cans in the parking lot."

The vice president responded, "Rachel, you've confirmed my good judgment in promoting you to a leadership position."

"Thanks, Gary, but why?" asked Rachel.

"Because you think big," said Gary. "You search for the implications of ordinary events. Another person would have looked at the litter and simply concluded that the maintenance people were not doing their job. Instead, you looked at the possible message indicated by the litter."

Popular wisdom is that to be a leader, the starting point is to look like a leader. Have good posture, be well groomed, wear clothing similar to that worn by leaders in a particular field, and smile frequently. However, you are much more likely to become a leader, or further develop as a leader, if you think like one.

Introduction

Welcome aboard the leadership train! Leadership in politics, government, sports, and business has always been an exciting topic. During the past decade, interest in business leadership has surged. Without effective leadership at all levels in organizations, it is difficult to sustain profitability, productivity, quality, and good customer service. In dozens of ways, leadership does make a difference.

Effective leadership is certainly good for entire organizations and their units (such as departments or divisions). The person providing the leadership can also get some goodies, such as higher status, pay, visibility, and a feeling of being an insider. Being a leader may have its headaches, but it is also glamorous.

If you want good insights and skills into leadership to supplement the many platitudes and evangelical statements that abound, you have come to the right place. My intent in this material is to help readers enhance their leadership effectiveness whether or not they currently occupy a formal leadership position.

Chapter 6

What Is Leadership?

In This Chapter

- What leadership really means
- The difference between leadership and management
- Effective leaders versus effective managers
- Leadership as a relationship and a partnership
- To lead is to inspire, persuade, influence, and motivate
- Leading changes and transformations

Imagine it's the end of your professional career and you're about to retire. You've been lucky enough to work for a company long enough to collect at least a small pension and participate in a retirement party. Which of the following toasts do you want the emcee to propose?

A. "_____ was a wonderful worker here and in the other six companies he (or she) worked for. Nobody heard a peep out of _____, yet we all admired _____ for being a quiet, behind-the-scenes worker bee."

B. "What an inspiring leader _____ was during six years of employment with us. I heard that _____ was also an inspiring leader at other phases in

> **Another Perspective**
> Leadership, of course, is not just for business. For many people the best opportunities for practicing leadership are in volunteer organizations, sports teams, and religious organizations.

his (or her) career. Long before _____ received the first of two promotions, we knew that _____ had the right stuff to be a leader."

To those of you who responded "B," keep reading. This material will get you started on the road to leadership, or if you're already somewhere along the way, you'll improve your present leadership capabilities.

A foundation step in developing your leadership ability is understanding the nature of leadership. It is difficult to do justice to the complexity of leadership with a one-sentence definition. This chapter will explain what leadership is and how it differs from management. You will also learn about the most important leadership activities—inspiring, persuading, influencing, and motivating.

What Leadership Really Means

Leadership, like love, can be explained in many different ways. Here are several definitions to get you started thinking like a leader:

1. Leadership is interpersonal influence directed toward attaining goals and is achieved through communication. By communication we refer simply to sending and receiving messages. According to this definition, a leader might stop by a person's cubicle and give her a word of encouragement about increasing her number of visits to influential dealers.
2. Leadership is a way of influencing people beyond routine compliance with directions and orders. A leader, for example, might influence workers to want to work beyond 40 hours per week so they can share in the glory of the success of the department.
3. Leadership is an act that causes others to act or respond in a shared direction. A leader, for example, might excite the group about trying to move in the same direction of improving quality.
4. Leadership is the key dynamic force that motivates and coordinates an organization to accomplish its objectives. Without being inspired by a leader, a total organization or a department might drift along with no careful focus on a key objective such as trying to improve worker safety.

5. Leadership is the ability to inspire confidence and support among the people who are needed to attain organizational goals. This is another way of stating the obvious—that the leader's job is to capture the cooperation of people who do the actual work in the organization.

> **Key Word**
> If people do not do anything differently from what they would have done without your presence, you have not exerted **leadership.**

A leader who can inspire, persuade, influence, and motivate can spearhead useful changes. Bringing about change is a critical leadership goal because most improvement requires a departure from the status quo. A leader creates a vision for others and then directs them toward achieving that vision. To be a leader, you must have followers who have confidence in you and who give you their support and commitment to a goal. This is what *leadership* really means.

So What's So Good About Being a Leader?

If being a leader didn't have loads of potential benefits, not so many people would want to become leaders. A key advantage of being a leader is that it gives you a feeling of power and prestige. The prestige comes from the fact that so many people admire leaders. Leaders are often in a wonderful position to help others, thereby finding their jobs satisfying. Part of helping others is making a contribution to society. A woman started a soccer league for poor city children. She claims that many of these children have avoided wrongdoing as her leagues have spread to forty cities. Imagine how good this woman feels.

Leadership positions pay well, with top corporate leaders earning about 150 times as much as entry-level workers. Being placed in a leadership position is also valuable because it is a good vantage point for further promotions. Leaders also enjoy the feeling of being in on things. As a leader, you are often privy to information excluded from others. Consider also that leaders have the satisfaction of controlling money in the form of budgets.

The Difference Between Leaders and Managers

To understand leadership, you must understand the difference between leadership and management. Management includes planning, organizing, leading, and controlling. Although leadership is part of a manager's job, a manager must spend time on the planning, organizing, and controlling functions. Leadership strives to accomplish change, whereas management focuses on maintaining equilibrium. An effective leader inspires people to work hard to improve profits; an effective manager makes sure people are adequately paid for their effort. Here are some differences between leadership and management:

- Management is more formal and scientific than leadership. It relies on foundation skills such as planning, controlling, and making effective use of information technology.
- Management uses an explicit set of tools and techniques, based on reasoning and testing, that you can apply to a variety of situations. Leadership has fewer explicit tools.
- Leadership requires eliciting teamwork and cooperation from a vast network of people and motivating a large number of people in that network.
- A leader frequently displays enthusiasm, passion, and inspiration to get others to attain high levels of performance. Managing involves less outward emotion and a more conservative demeanor to achieve goals once they are defined.

Key Word

A **vision** is an idealized scenario of the future of an organization—a goal that entices people to work toward a rosy future. A **leader** creates the vision and a strategy to reach the vision; a **manager** uses a set of skills to work toward achieving the vision.

Watch Out!

Although it's important to appreciate the differences between leadership and management, don't go overboard. Taking the differences to the extreme, the leader becomes an inspirational figure up in the clouds and the manager becomes a plodding bureaucrat mired in the status quo.

- A leader makes frequent use of his or her imagination and creative problem-solving techniques to bring about change. A manager tends to make frequent use of standard, well-established solutions to problems.
- The key contribution of the *leader* is creating a *vision* for the organization. The leader specifies the far-reaching goal as well as the strategy for reaching that goal. The key contribution of the *manager* is implementing the vision.

Avoid the trendy thinking that leadership is so important, it turns management into an insignificant activity. Although people need to be inspired, persuaded, influenced, and motivated, they still need to be well managed. Leadership is an integral part of management but not a substitute for it. The world vitally needs both good leaders and good managers. Many exceptional leaders are also exceptional managers, such as Louis Gerstner who spearheaded the resurgence of IBM.

Advisor

If you are committed to becoming a leader or improving your leadership stature, make every day count. Today, leadership could mean contributing a sparkling idea at a meeting. Tomorrow, it could mean giving a warm smile and a handshake to the new entry-level worker assigned to your team. Two days from now, your act of leadership might be to show a coworker how she can improve her productivity without putting in more hours on the job.

A Leader Is a Manager

A disturbing implication of some of the current writing on leadership is that being a leader is *good* whereas being a manager is *bad*. I want you to appreciate the wonders of leadership, but I do not want to denigrate the importance of management. Remember that a leader is also a manager. Following a framework that has stood the test of time, a manager plans, organizes, controls, and leads. Especially in a business environment, a leader is also supposed to carry out the other functions of management.

An Example of a Leader and Manager

Take a look at a person who is one of the business world's best leaders *and* managers, Larry Bossidy, CEO of Allied Signal. Although not a household name, the company is a giant auto parts and aerospace conglomerate. Before being recruited into his present position, Bossidy honed his leadership and management skills at General Electric, working as the number-two executive behind the legendary Jack Welch.

Bossidy inspires his managers with his charismatic presence and his insistence on growth. Growing a business is a definitive act of leadership. As a leader, he is brutally demanding and readily fires managers who cannot meet his targets for growth or return on invested capital. Bossidy is at his best simplifying complex issues for people and giving them clear targets. For example, here are three of his strategies for growth:

1. **Cut the fat.** This is the first step in boosting productivity; only the lean grow profitably.
2. **Set killer goals.** Targets that make people stretch to reach them motivate people better than reasonable ones.
3. **Claw your way to victory.** No excuses. Push managers relentlessly to meet your growth goals.

As a leader, Bossidy inspires people with his formidable presence and his extraordinary goals. As a manager, he carefully develops plans and, wherever feasible, prunes costs. The way he handles acquisitions illustrates his managerial aplomb. Bossidy avoids giant takeovers. Instead, he opts for small, readily digestible acquisitions that fit a niche in his product line, such as adding a windshield-wiper blade manufacturer to Allied Signal's auto parts group. This acclaimed leader has successfully combined high-level leadership and management skills.

An Example of a Leader Who Is Not a Manager

When a leader neglects being a good manager, the results can be disastrous. Bob, a former vice president in an advertising agency, has many good leadership qualities, but he is a poor manager. As a result, his credibility diminished to the point where he lost his leadership effectiveness.

Bob inspired people with his warmth, charm, and creativity. He could line up subcontractors for major projects, dazzling them with promises of riches and glory if they would undertake projects for his firm. Clients were mesmerized by his intellectual energy and creative suggestions—both important aspects of leadership.

As a manager, Bob was disorganized and had poor follow-through. Agreements with subcontractors were often broken. When he did keep a promise, the subcontractors (for example, a small advertising agency) often had to struggle to obtain their advances. Bob was too disorganized to effectively delegate the details. Even worse, he often forgot what he had told people.

Bob's problems had many causes: He did not seriously understand the capabilities of his firm; he did not ask for enough input from the people in his command; he did not find out what each person could contribute. Even when he did have an accurate idea of what his team could accomplish, he did not pay attention to *when* they could accomplish it. As a result, Bob frustrated both his team members and his clients. As complaints about his performance accumulated, Bob was eventually invited out of the advertising agency.

> **Advisor**
>
> You might be an inspiring, charismatic leader who consistently motivates others to peaks of performance. Even if you are, you still need to back up your leadership ability with planning, organizing, and controlling. An inspiring leader can sometimes squeeze by with an executive assistant or assistant manager who acts as a strong backup. However, keep in mind that a leader needs enough managerial skills to make effective use of the managerial skills of others.

A Leader Is Involved in a Partnership

Another way of understanding leadership is to think of it as both a relationship and a partnership between the leader and the group members. Forming a partnership depends upon building a relationship. You, as the leader, relate to others similarly to the way you relate to family members and friends. Instead of being detached and distant, you have rapport with and good feelings about group members.

Think of the difference in how you interact with people while riding a shuttle bus in an airport versus riding in a car pool van. During your ride at the airport, you probably relate very little to the people around you, except for the exchange of a few pleasantries. If you are a member of a van pool, you probably develop a relationship with each person in the van.

The term partnership reflects the relatively equal power between the leader and all of his or her constituents. Leaders who are partners of group members welcome their partners' input. As a leader, you can still provide direction and inspiration while regarding partners as group members rather than employees or subordinates. For a valid partnership to exist, the following conditions must be met:

- The leader develops a vision only after receiving input from his or her partners.
- Group members have the right to disagree with the leader and are regarded as valuable contributors to the group effort.
- Both the leader and the group members are held accountable for results. If the group members want to be treated as partners, they have to risk being accountable for failures as well as accomplishments.
- The leader and the group members are honest with each other. Not telling the truth is a violation of the implied contract between the leader and the group members.
- The leader and the group members recognize that squabbles are inevitable, as they are in most partnerships. In an effective partnership, most of the squabbles are resolved in an equitable fashion instead of being left to fester.

Given that leadership is a partnership, the leader and the group members have serious responsibilities toward each other. Each member of the group, the leader included, feels a personal responsibility for achieving the group's mission. For the partnership to work, open communication must flow about good news and bad news. You can tell a leader has a good partnership when a group member can say to the leader without fear of retribution, "I just screwed up and I need your help." Similarly, the leader should be able to say to a team member, "You've made what I consider to be a big mistake. And I want to help you fix the problem."

Advisor

A useful mental set for improving your leadership effectiveness is to think of yourself and your work group as partners in a small business. As the leader, you may be the partner with the biggest stake in the business, yet everyone is striving for success and is dependent upon everyone else. If you cannot trust your partners, and if they cannot trust you, your enterprise is in big trouble.

How Good Are You at Inspiring, Persuading, Influencing, and Motivating?

A leader is a person who inspires, persuades, influences, and motivates others. These are the basics of leadership. How do you accomplish these actions? Here are a few examples to illustrate what I mean by inspiration, persuasion, influence, and motivation.

Inspiration

The ability to inspire others represents the highest form of leadership. A leader must usually have a magnetic personality or set a wonderful example (or both) to inspire others. Consider these two scenarios:

1. Cheryl has been going about her job in a mundane manner for several years. She gets the job done but never works at her capacity or brings forth an exceptional idea. A new manager, Nick, is appointed to the unit. Nick's excitement about his work and the emotional support he gives group members create a change in Cheryl's attitude. Cheryl now strives to perform the best she can and contributes imaginative ideas for increasing productivity.
2. Max has been on a career plateau for several years. He hasn't received a promotion or a higher salary in three years. Max blames office politics for both conditions. A new supervisor, Jennifer, is appointed to Max's unit. Jennifer takes an interest in Max and listens carefully to his tale of woe. Jennifer also challenges Max to take more responsibility for his career stagnation. A light flashes in Max's mind. He is inspired to take several courses to earn a certificate in his field. This enhances his credentials for a promotion or

salary upgrade. Jennifer also influences Max by her own positive approach to self-development. She reads career-related publications and attends professional seminars.

> **Watch Out!**
> When you are busy carrying out your managerial responsibilities day-by-day, it is easy to neglect actions that merit the term leadership. Avoid the trap of getting so caught up in conducting routine transactions with others that you neglect to inspire, persuade, influence, or motivate them. To be a leader, you have to modify the behavior of your target people in some way.

The two managers just described did an effective job of influencing group members to make positive changes. Keep this in mind as a guiding principle when leading others.

Persuasion

Persuasion is another key aspect of a leader's role. A leader must often get people to change their minds or take an action they had not considered.

Amy, a leader in an appliance manufacturing company, observes that several of her supervisors are not making good use of the information technology available to them. For example, when they need information about parts and shipments, they make a series of phone calls and personal visits. Amy wants to encourage them to use the company intranet instead.

Amy sits down with the supervisors, individually and collectively, to present the arguments for using the company's network. Her logical persuasion works. The supervisors then ask for coaching on the new network system. Amy did not have to resort to threats or punishment. She *led* the supervisors by means of persuasion.

Influence

Influence is almost synonymous with leadership. Leadership is often defined as the process of influencing others to achieve objectives. A leader in a work setting influences group members to accomplish such things as

- Taking on more responsibility as tasks are redistributed after a company downsizing.
- Shooting for higher quality standards when there are too many defects in the current product or service.
- Raising corporate ethical standards in dealing with customers, suppliers, and coworkers.

In all three instances, the leader influenced a team member to do something positive that helped the organization. Many leaders, unfortunately, influence group members to engage in negative, unethical acts that hurt the organization in the long term. An example would be lying about possible delivery dates, or making false claims about the firm's capabilities.

Key Word
An objective can originate from your group. The group members might say, for example, "We want to be the most outstanding credit department in the entire organization." As the leader, you **influence** the group in achieving this objective.

Motivation

Motivation is also part of the nuts and bolts of a leader's job. To motivate another person is to somehow get that person to put added effort into the job. Motivation is a perennial challenge built into the leadership part of a manager's job. Motivation refers to actual behavior—not promises or fantasies! It is easy to be deceived by the glib-talking group member who describes in glowing terms how he or she wants to become a superior performer. This person might also share dreams of becoming a senior vice president. The first evidence that you have motivated that person is when he or she works harder than usual on today's tasks.

Leaders Accomplish Big Changes

One more defining characteristic of a leader for now: An effective leader brings about change and transformation. The major justification for paying top-level business leaders so much more than other workers is that the leaders spearhead constructive change. Effective leaders typically feel uncomfortable with the status quo. They ask themselves such questions as

- "What's broken that needs fixing?"
- "What is working okay but could stand some improvement?"
- "What is so sacred about our standard way of handling this?"
- "What changes would help us rise above the competition?"
- "Why doesn't our company have a better reputation?"
- "What changes would elevate us to a level of excellence?"

Leaders who can ask and find answers to the last question are classified as transformational leaders. They bring about sweeping, positive changes in organizations. Keep in mind that becoming a transformational leader is the ideal you want to achieve.

The Least You Need to Know

- Leaders influence people to follow a course of action through persuasion or example.
- As a leader, you form constructive relationships and partnerships with people.
- Effective leaders inspire, persuade, influence, and motivate others and spearhead useful changes.
- Leaders transform mediocre organizations into excellent organizations.

Chapter 7

Build Your Self-Confidence

In This Chapter

- Why self-confidence is important for leadership
- Thinking positive thoughts
- Taking an inventory of your assets
- Revving up your need for power
- Obtaining a few easy victories first
- Bouncing back from setbacks

Assume you are a manager in a company rumored to be facing bankruptcy. At a company-wide meeting, the CEO sobs, "I'm sorry. I'm just no good in a crisis. I don't think I can get us out of this mess. Maybe one of you would like to try your hand at turning around a troubled company."

In a situation such as this, employees feel insecure. The people you manage would be so preoccupied with finding new employment that they wouldn't be able to concentrate on their work. You yourself would want the president to behave in a confident, reassuring manner. On the other hand, if the president acted arrogant, or if he or she treated the crisis lightly, you might not feel secure either.

In this chapter, I give you detailed advice about how you can build up the right amount of self-confidence to become an effective leader. Building self-confidence represents an excellent foundation for becoming an effective leader. Almost all successful leaders are self-confident.

Why Self-Confidence Is Important

In most leadership situations, the leader who functions best is self-confident enough to appear in control and reassure others. However, if a leader is so self-confident that he or she does not admit errors, listen to criticism, or ask for advice, this situation creates a problem.

> **Key Word**
> Self-efficacy is akin to being self-confident about your ability to execute a task. For example, have you ever had a computer file apparently disappear into cyberspace? A person with high self-efficacy on retrieving lost files might move right into the temporary file bin and retrieve the file you thought was lost forever.

Developing or strengthening your self-confidence is a foundation for improving your leadership ability. Self-confidence and leadership feed upon one another. If people perceive you as self-confident, they are likely to accept you as a leader. As people accept you as a leader, your self-confidence increases. In turn, you meet with greater acceptance as a leader, followed by yet another small boost in self-confidence.

A large helping of self-confidence is also important because it contributes to your own belief in your capability to perform a task—referred to as *self-efficacy*. People with a heightened sense of self-efficacy tend to have good job performance. They also set lofty goals for themselves. Self-efficacy contributes to leadership effectiveness: A leader with high self-efficacy believes that a task is doable. As a result, this leader can inspire others to carry out a difficult mission—for example, correcting a serious customer problem.

Use Positive Self-Talk

To appear self-confident and to project a strong leadership image, positive self-talk must replace negative self-talk. Positive self-talk means saying positive things about yourself to yourself. Positive self-talkers also make positive statements about themselves when speaking to others. If your manager asks you to take on a difficult assignment, use positive self-talk and say, "Let me give it a shot. My track record in dealing with the near-impossible has been good so far."

The biggest leadership dividends from positive self-talk come when positive self-talk takes place in front of others. Read the following steps to get started on using positive self-talk. Self-discipline is needed to implement these seven steps successfully. Choose an incident or a quality you want to amend and apply each step to that incident or quality. Repeat this exercise often throughout the week to get this new habit of positive self-talk established in your mind:

1. Objectively state the incident that is creating doubt about your capabilities. The key word here is "objectively." Chris, who is fearful of his ability to conduct a customer satisfaction survey for the company, might say, "I've been asked to conduct a customer satisfaction survey for the company, and I'm not good at conducting surveys."
2. Objectively interpret what the incident *does not* mean. Chris might say, "Not being skilled at conducting a survey doesn't mean that I can't figure out a way to do a useful survey or that I'm an ineffective employee."
3. Objectively state what the incident *does* mean. To implement this step, you should avoid put-down labels such as incompetent, stupid, dumb, jerk, or airhead. All these terms are forms of negative self-talk. At this point, Chris should state what the incident is really about: "I have a problem with one small aspect of this job—conducting a customer survey. This means I need to acquire skills in conducting a survey."
4. Objectively account for the cause of the incident. Chris might say, "I'm really worried about conducting an accurate survey because I have very little experience of this nature."
5. Identify some positive thoughts to prevent your fear of the incident from recurring. Chris could say, "I'll buy a book on conducting surveys and follow it carefully," or "I'll enroll in a seminar on conducting customer surveys."
6. Use positive self-talk in an interaction. Chris imagines his boss saying, "This survey is really good. I'm proud of my decision to select you to conduct this important survey." When the opportunity arises, Chris will respond to his boss, "I'm glad you asked me to conduct the survey. I'm eager to take on new challenges, and I've done well with them in the past." Or Chris might say, "Thanks for the opportunity for professional growth."

7. This final step is important in keeping the momentum going. It is a general application of positive self-talk rather than applying it to a specific incident: Start each day with positive thoughts. Positive self-talk is a complex habit that requires frequent reinforcement and reinvigoration. Invest at least five minutes each day in creating constructive energy. Just before launching the day's activities is a good time for this exercise. Find a quiet place free from interruptions, get comfortable, breathe deeply, and think positive thoughts. Tell yourself that you can meet any professional or personal challenges that life has to offer. Think about your recent positive accomplishments and all the compliments you have received in the last 30 days.

Eliminate Negative Self-Talk

The flip side of developing positive self-talk is to avoid negative self-talk. To boost your self-confidence, minimize negative statements about yourself to others. You will appear more like a leader. The following statements reveal a lack of self-confidence:

> "I may be stupid, but..." or "Nobody asked my opinion," or "I know I'm usually wrong, but..." or "I know I don't have as much education as some people, but..."

Self-effacing statements such as these serve to reinforce low self-confidence. Instead, regard your weak points as areas for possible self-improvement. Negative self-labeling can do long-term damage to your self-confidence and leadership ability.

Advisor

Suppose you have mastered the art of self-talk, and you begin to get vibes that you are irritating others with your image of perfection. Throw in an occasional self-effacing comment just to humanize yourself. You might say, "My 13-year-old told me he would teach me how to use my digital camera any day now." Remember that your goal is to increase the ratio of positive self-affirmations to negative ones, not to glow like an announcer on a home-shopping network!

You've Got More Going for You Than You Thought

Many people suffer from low self-confidence because they do not appreciate their own good points. A basic tactic for increasing your self-confidence is to take an inventory of personal assets and accomplishments. Create an asset list to help you recognize what you already have. Most people who do not feel confident about themselves overlook their many good points.

For this exercise, personal assets should be related to characteristics and behaviors, rather than tangible assets such as property and investments. Accomplishments can be anything significant where you played a key role in achieving the results. Don't be modest in preparing your list of assets and accomplishments. You are looking for any confidence-booster you can find.

Two asset lists prepared by two different people will give you an idea of the kinds of assets and accomplishments you can include.

Wanda's Asset List

Good listener

Good problem-solver

Better-than-average information technology skills

Most people like me

Assertive in work and social situations

Inquisitive mind

Patient with people who make mistakes

Good conflict-resolution skills

Good posture

Good sense of humor

Better-than-average appearance

Excellent dancer

Organized successful fund drive that raised $50,000 for church

Graduated 20th in college class of 350

Captain of league-winning volleyball team

Mother of two well-adjusted, happy children

Angelo's Asset List

Good analytical skills

Excellent computer skills

Good sales skills

Work well under pressure

Known for dependability and follow-through

Good dancer

Expert skier

Good cook

Excellent physical appearance

Humble when necessary

Made award-winning suggestion that saved company $100,000 in first year

Made winning run in ski meet that enabled my team to place first

Gave CPR that saved life of auto accident victim

First person in family to graduate from college

The value of these asset lists is that they add to your self-appreciation. Most people who write down their good points come away from the activity with at least a temporary boost in self-confidence. The temporary boost, combined with a few successful experiences, can lead to a long-term gain in self-confidence. Be sure to add to your list whenever you accomplish or learn something new.

An important supplement to listing your own assets is hearing the opinion of others about your good points. This tactic must be used sparingly, however, and mainly with people like you who are interested in personal growth. A good icebreaker is to tell someone you think will be receptive that you want to create a list of your assets for a leadership-development exercise. Choose a person who knows your work or capabilities and ask whether he or she can spare a few moments for this important experience.

> **Advisor**
>
> For many people, hearing positive feedback from others does more toward building self-confidence than recording feedback from yourself. The reason is that self-esteem depends to a large extent on what we think other people think about us. Consequently, if other people—whose judgment you trust—think highly of you, your self-image will be positive. Heightened self-esteem and self-image contribute mightily to your self-confidence.

Rev Up Your Need for Power

A thirst for *power* is a distinguishing characteristic of successful leaders in business and other fields. In other words, they crave to control resources. Leaders with high power needs have four dominant characteristics:

1. They act with vigor and determination to exercise their power.
2. They invest time in thinking about ways to alter the behavior and thinking of others.
3. They care about their status in comparison with the people around them.
4. They regard power as one of life's most precious commodities.

These characteristics of the power-oriented person can be developed. It's a question of thinking through each item and saying to yourself, "Is this really true of my thinking?" Next, remind yourself of your new power attitude from time to time. As you watch a long private yacht sailing down river or bay, say to yourself, "Ahh yes. Power is good."

> **Key Word**
>
> The ability or potential to influence decisions and control resources is a mark of **power.** Power is required to exercise influence over others as, for example, in getting others to part with resources such as money.

How is power linked to self-confidence? As a person becomes more powerful—acquires more power—he or she grows in self-confidence. It does wonders for your self-confidence when others extend themselves to do favors for you because they perceive you as powerful. The link between power and self-confidence runs in both directions. Power adds to self-confidence, and self-confidence helps you acquire power. If people perceive you as self-confident, they also perceive you as having a powerful personality. A powerful personality, of course, adds to your leadership stature.

How Strong Is Your Need for Power?

To develop a tentative analysis of your need for power, see how many of the following statements you agree with. The more you agree with, the more likely it is that you already have a strong power need:

1. I would like to have a high school or hospital named after me.
2. Power is exciting and wonderful.
3. If I could, I would like to include the rich and the famous as my friends.
4. I wish I could have a huge, beautifully decorated office at the top floor of an office tower.
5. It would thrill me to see my photo on the front page of *Time, Business Week, Fortune,* or any other national magazine.
6. I would like to have a large staff ready to carry out my directions at a moment's notice.
7. A fancy title is very important to me.
8. It would thrill me if an Internet search engine came up with 75,000 listings under my name.
9. I think that power adds to a person's sex appeal.
10. It would feel great if strangers greeted me by name in public places.

> **Watch Out!**
> Be aware that an extreme need for power can backfire. Craving power can lead to unethical, immoral, and illegal acts. A person obsessed with power may back-stab rivals. Some power-obsessed people become paranoid, on guard against people they perceive as threats. Have you ever heard of a powerful person who maintained an "enemies list" of people to disparage and harm at the right moment?

I want you to concentrate on cultivating your *need* for power. My logic is that if you develop a strong need for power, you boost your self-confidence. An important contributing factor is that a person who craves power develops a power presence. Your craving for power, within ethical and legal limits, makes you appear self-confident.

Concentrate now on enhancing your desire for power. If you already have a strong power need, you can work through this section quickly. However, you might pick up a few ideas for further solidifying your power motive. Begin by imagining some of the potential benefits of being powerful.

People will attempt to curry favor with you. Think of all those people smiling at you when you enter the office. You are likely to earn a well-above-average income, thus alleviating or eliminating any financial problems you may have.

You will feel "in on things" as people feed you more inside information because they perceive you as powerful. You will be able to savor tidbits of information about such events as plans for expanding or downsizing.

You will be able to control money and other organizational resources. Even though you may not be able to spend the money personally, you will get satisfaction from knowing that your judgment on financial matters is trusted.

You will receive respect from a wide range of people who appreciate power. As a direct result, your prestige will increase. You will gain status both for your power and the leadership position that will most likely accompany your power. You will have the opportunity to help others. Power gives a person the resources to help others. A powerful person, for example, might be able to find a job for someone in need of employment.

Visualize a More Powerful You

Another step in revving up your need for power is to visualize what it would be like to be more powerful. Sit back, relax, and get your imagination going. Create a videotape in your mind of yourself becoming more powerful. Imagine enjoying some of the benefits you just read about.

Think of men and women wanting to open doors for you. See yourself walking into a meeting a few minutes late and the other participants stopping their chatter to greet you. Picture yourself choosing whatever

> **Watch Out!**
> Sometimes when people start thinking like this, they may develop the bad habit of actually believing they are better than others and expect others to defer to them. This is a big mistake. What you want is for people to respect you because they know you have their best interests in mind as well as your own and therefore want to defer to you rather than feeling they are required to do so.

clothing you want to wear without considering the price. Imagine decorating your office in almost any way you choose, including art from around the world.

Create a visual image of various people asking your opinion on different topics and listening carefully even if what you have to say is nothing more than common sense.

Think of crowds of people wanting to shake your hand, or tap you on the arm, because they are attracted by your powerful presence. Imagine the sights, sound, taste, and touch of power.

Grab a Few Easy Victories

Self-confidence accumulates with a variety of successes, so start with relatively easy tasks. Suppose you want to submit ideas to your company that will create substantial change and give you a surge in prestige and recognition. You realize that the probability of getting a breakthrough idea accepted is small. A good way to build self-confidence is to first make several small suggestions that are likely to be accepted. For example, a research analyst in a financial services firm suggested that data-entry people use a paper holder to reduce neck strain when entering data on their computers. This simple suggestion meant that workers would suffer less and worker compensation claims (and insurance premiums) might be reduced. After this suggestion was successfully implemented, the research analyst made bolder suggestions for ergonomic redesign in the office.

A variation of the easy-victory strategy is to place yourself in a less competitive environment, especially if you find that you are in over your head in your present environment. It's bad for your self-confidence to keep getting clobbered. A less competitive environment—such as working with more cooperative coworkers—might be just what you need to establish a satisfactory level of self-confidence.

Advisor

The tactic "win a few easy victories" works well because it is based on the success cycle. Each little success builds your self-confidence, which leads to a bigger success, which leads to more self-confidence, and so on.

After obtaining several easy victories, move on to bigger challenges. Small accomplishments are important because they pave the way to tackling more complex activities. A person who aspires to be a restaurant owner might work first as an assistant manager, and then as manager, of someone else's restaurant. If you achieve something that stretches your capability, that achievement serves as objective evidence that you are a capable—and therefore confident—individual. As a result, you strengthen an important leadership characteristic.

Bounce Back from Setbacks and Embarrassments

One of the best self-confidence builders is to convince yourself that you can conquer adversity such as setbacks and embarrassments. The vast majority of successful leaders have dealt successfully with at least one significant setback in their career, such as being fired or demoted. In contrast, crumbling after a setback or series of setbacks usually lowers your self-confidence. Following are two major suggestions for bouncing back from setbacks and embarrassments.

Get Past the Emotional Turmoil

Adversity has enormous emotional consequences. The emotional impact of severe job adversity can rival the loss of a personal relationship. The stress from adversity leads to a cycle of adversity followed by stress, followed by more adversity. The following tactics can help you cope successfully with the emotional aspects of adversity:

- **Accept the reality of your problem.** Dealing constructively with the emotional aspects of a crisis does not mean denying the reality of your problem. Admit that your problems are real and that you are hurting inside.
- **Do not take the setback personally.** Remember that setbacks are inevitable as long as you are taking some risks in your career. Not personalizing setbacks helps reduce some of the emotional sting.
- **Don't panic.** Recognize that you are in a difficult circumstance under which many others would panic. Convince yourself to remain calm enough to deal with the problem or crisis, no matter how severe.
- **Get help from your support network.** After interviewing hundreds of people about how they bounced back from career and personal setbacks, I reached an important conclusion: Getting emotional support from family members and friends helps people overcome the emotional turmoil associated with adversity. No other

technique was even a close second to talking out your problems with a trusted listener.

Learning how to bounce back from adversity can be a major step forward in your quest to build your career as a leader, or any other type of work. Not being able to shake loose from adversity is debilitating.

Find a Creative Solution to Your Problem

An inescapable part of planning a comeback is to solve your problem. Typically, an off-the-shelf-solution is not available. Instead, you need to search for creative alternatives. Here is a widely used problem-solving method:

> **Another Perspective**
>
> Finding a creative alternative solution to the adverse problem you face lies at the heart of being resilient. The owner of a printing company faced difficult times. With so many customers owning desk-top publishing and high-speed duplicating equipment, his business was suffering. He needed time to regroup and cash to tide the business over for the intermediate range. The creative alternative he chose was to sell the company building and lease it back. Proceeds from the sale gave the business the necessary infusion of cash for survival.

1. **Diagnose and clarify the problem.** What is the real problem created by your adversity? Are you suffering losses in income, self-esteem, job satisfaction, personal relationships, and well-being (or any combination of the preceding)?
2. **Search for creative alternatives.** What options are open? To be resilient, you may have to find a creative solution to your problem.
3. **Make a choice.** If your career crisis is to be resolved, you must make a tough decision at some point.
4. **Develop an action plan and implement it.** What steps must you take to get out of this mess?
5. **Evaluate outcomes.** Did your recovery plan work or will you have to try another alternative? Within six months, you usually know whether you made a workable choice.

Being able to work through tough problems is a powerful elixir for low self-confidence. If your self-confidence is already high, it will continue to strengthen as you solve more problems successfully.

The Least You Need to Know

- Think positive thoughts about yourself.
- Write down your good points to boost your self-confidence.
- Visualize a more powerful you.
- Follow a few easy victories with bigger challenges.
- Deal creatively with the emotional turmoil associated with adversity.

Chapter 8

How Do Leaders Think?

In This Chapter

- Making good use of your intuition
- How to look at the big picture
- How and when to ask tough questions
- Learning to be more creative and innovative
- How to become a more penetrating thinker
- How to read people better

Michelle had four years of experience as a manufacturing engineer when she decided to apply for a job as a production supervisor at another company. At the end of her first interview, the hiring manager asked, "Michelle, do you have any other questions?"

Michelle responded, "Oh yes, I do. I had to drive 25 miles to come to this interview. How many cents per mile will I be reimbursed?"

After Michelle left, the hiring manager wrote down on his yellow pad: "Generally good candidate, but I question her ability to think like a leader. She focuses on trivial details. Doesn't see the big picture."

In this chapter, you will learn the value of thinking big and how to adopt the thinking pattern of leaders. This information is extremely important. The mental side of leadership can contribute as much to leadership effectiveness as personality.

Trust Your Gut Feelings

A major part of a leader's job is to make decisions, both big and small. Intuition is a key personal trait many leaders rely on to make good decisions. *Intuition* is an experience-based way of knowing or reasoning in which weighing and balancing the evidence are done automatically. Effective leaders do not rely on analytical and data-driven techniques alone. They also rely heavily on hunches and intuition. Using this method, the decision-maker arrives at a conclusion without using the step-by-step logical process.

Being intuitive generally means that you rely heavily on the right half of the brain. The left half of the brain controls analytical thinking, whereas the right half controls creative and intuitive thinking. Effective decision-makers achieve a balance between analytical and intuitive, or left-brain and right-brain, thinking. Rather than operate independently of each other, the analytical and intuitive approaches should be complementary aspects of decision-making.

> **Key Word**
> Trusting your **intuition**, you might arrive at a sudden insight or solution to a problem without having to evaluate the facts. You will not have to systematically weigh the pros and cons of the possibilities you are facing.

A strong leader knows when to rely on intuition and when to be more analytical. You could say that a strong leader intuitively knows when to use intuition and when to use careful analysis!

Intuition can be developed and sharpened, although it won't happen overnight. Enhancing your intuition is like sharpening your common sense. In fact, intuition incorporates common sense. If you are willing to make the effort to become a more intuitive thinker, keep the following suggestions in mind:

- **Immerse yourself.** Get plenty of experience in the area where you want to become more intuitive and exercise leadership. An experienced leader, for example, might have good intuition about just how far to stretch group members with demanding goals. One of the reasons he or she knows the limits is because he or she faced a similar situation 50 or more times.

- **Get tuned in.** Stay carefully attuned to those little sensations inside your body when you make a decision. In fact, the term "gut feeling" means that you are carefully attuned to the physiological signs of emotion within your body. You know that your gut (intestine) is telling you something because you have a curious internal rumbling or flutter. This little sign is a signal that your thoughts are creating an emotional response. Your gut reaction often suggests to you "Go forward" or "Watch out."
- **Lend an ear.** Listen carefully when that little voice inside your brain says, "This is the right move!" or "This is the wrong move!" If you don't listen now, you may be plagued later with the thought, "I should have listened to my instincts."
- **Focus.** Concentrate on the task at hand so that you can be more aware of your intuition. The challenge is to put aside distracting problems before you enter an important decision-making situation. For example, clear out your e-mail inbox before tackling a demanding situation such as negotiating with a vendor or conducting a performance appraisal.
- **Log your successes.** Maintain a log of the accuracy of your intuitive decisions. When you trust your hunches, record the nature of the hunch and, later on, whether it proved to be accurate. For example, "On July 1, I predicted, without benefit of market research, that our two-headed ice scraper would be a big hit. I was right on target." Getting feedback on the accuracy of your forecasts enables you to fine-tune your intuition.

Watch Out!
I have been touting the importance of intuition for effective leadership. Do not think, however, that all leadership decision-making is "shoot from the hip." In many instances, especially when dealing with unfamiliar territory, you will still want to sift through the evidence bit-by-bit before making a decision.

To reinforce what I have been saying, intuition comes about from a combination of judgment and experience. Keep practicing making decisions and your intuition will sharpen.

Start Seeing the Big Picture

As the anecdote at the beginning of this chapter implied, thinking big is part of being a leader. Leaders are supposed to see the broad implications of almost every action they or their group members take.

Strategic Thinking

Seeing the big picture is part of thinking strategically—a requirement for executive leadership. *Strategic thinking* is the ability to think in terms of how your actions help the organization adapt to the outside world. It also involves understanding the long-range implications of your thinking. Monroe Muffler and Brake, a fast-growing automotive services company, illustrates an effective adaptation to the outside world. Originally their main line of business was to install brakes and exhaust systems for individual consumers. However, company leaders began to realize that many of their customers were too busy to bother making separate trips for muffler and brake repair at Monroe, and routine auto servicing (such as an oil change) elsewhere. Monroe therefore added routine service to capture more business. Adapting to the outside world meant catering to the needs of busy customers.

> **Key Word**
> Hiring a highly competent supervisor to help strengthen the organization is a mark of **strategic thinking.**

Systems Thinking

Another way of understanding what it means to perceive the overall picture is to become a *systems thinker*. The systems thinker attempts to grasp how a change introduced in one part of the system (or organization) creates changes in the other parts of the system as well. The systems thinker also attempts to forecast how a change today will affect the company in the future.

> **Key Word**
> A **systems thinker** understands how any change implemented at one place in the firm creates changes in the rest of the firm as well, immediately and in the future.

Assume that the director of marketing pushes for total customer satisfaction. One change initiated in the organization triggers another change, resulting in the type of chain reaction that follows:

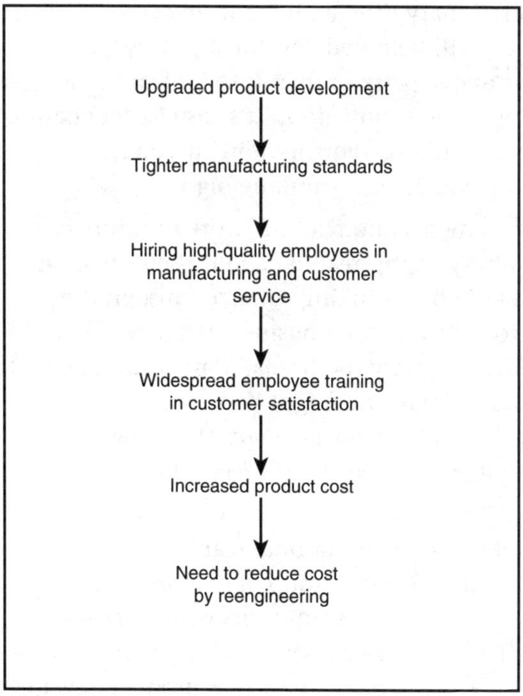

Chain of Consequences in an Organizational System.

Big Thinking

A person who is a little thinker must work diligently to become a big thinker. It's about as easy as a pessimist becoming an optimist! Yet it can be accomplished. Start with an *awareness* of the need for thinking big. Combine your new awareness with diligent *practice*. Here are a few suggestions to help you develop your new habit:

- Attempt to stop thinking little, especially with respect to giving high priority to your own self-interest. Imagine a person working in an office supply store 30 years ago. He hears that a company will start selling a newfangled machine that makes photocopies. Instead of imagining the positive implications for his company, he says, "That new Xerox machine will hurt my sales of carbon paper. I'll write a letter to the CEO telling him that almost nobody will choose photocopies over carbon paper." A big thinker would have said, "A revolution in office supplies might be on the horizon. What can I do to join this revolution? What supplies will people need to make photocopies?"

- Spend some of your discretionary time with big thinkers rather than little thinkers. Big thinkers will help you develop a positive, broad outlook because they rise above petty problems to look at the long-range goal. Little thinking can be contagious; it's easy to get channeled into a mode of little thinking. (Furthermore, if you don't agree with me, it's because you are not thinking big.)
- Study company vision statements and read the work of futurists. Even if futurists are not always right, reading about their forecasts will help elevate the level of your thinking. Glance through the *Harvard Business Review* for articles about business strategy. Get in touch with the World Future Society (Bethesda, Maryland). The best source of information about the future might be a newsletter published by Jossey-Bass Inc., *The Future at Work: Managing Forces that are Reshaping Organizations and Our Work Lives*. Also, check out "futurists" on the Web.
- See if you can be assigned to a cross-functional team within your firm. A cross-functional team is a small group of employees from different units who work together on specific problems and projects such as product development. Working with these people will help you appreciate how your work affects them.
- Imagine yourself wearing different company hats. If you are concerned about the quality of your product, imagine yourself wearing a "manufacturing hat." Tomorrow you may notice that your department is spending money too freely, so don your "finance hat." Next Monday, you might observe that several of your group members are struggling to balance family and work demands. Off the shelf comes your "human resources hat."

> **Watch Out!**
> In your quest to be a big thinker, do not neglect the important details that enable your company to run smoothly. Remember that a good leader is also a good manager. An effective big thinker combines systems thinking with a daily concern for running a tight ship.

Why and When to Ask Tough Questions

Strong leaders might not always have the right answers, but they usually have the right questions. A hard-hitting part of a leader's job is to ask tough questions. A *tough question* is one that makes a person or group stop and think about why they are doing or not doing something. In this way, group members are forced to think about the effectiveness of their activities.

Why Should I Ask a Tough Question?

The purpose of a tough question is not to intimidate, cajole, or belittle another person—but to help that person think through whether the status quo is good enough. A tough question often sets the stage for creative thinking because it questions whether an accepted practice could be radically changed. The beauty of a tough question is that it encourages people to ask themselves, "Why didn't I think of that? It seems so obvious."

Here's an example of asking a tough question. One of the leading companies in the garbage disposal field embarked on a program that lets customers pay their bills with a direct transfer of funds from their banks to the bank of the waste removal company. Consumers receive a statement every two months. The statement notes that the person is not required to send a payment but that the amount owed will be deducted from the customer's bank account.

> CAUTION
>
> **Watch Out!**
> Ask your tough questions after the warm-up phase of a meeting has been completed. People respond better to tough questions after they are already moving toward serious thinking. You might lose the potential good effect of a tough question if it is asked before people are mentally ready to think in depth.

A top manager at the waste disposal company had a neighbor who used the system. Out of curiosity, the manager asked to see the billing statement. She noted that it included a payment envelope and discovered that an envelope was included with each statement. Checking within the company, the manager learned that including the envelope was standard practice on all customer statements—whether they were pay by mail or by bank transfer.

The manager then asked a tough question: "Why are we sending payment envelopes to customers who do not use them? Are we trying to help the envelope company?" This prompted the manager of information systems to develop a routine that prevents including wasted envelopes with customer statements.

A tough question can also ask another person or group why they have *not* thought of something. Here are a few more examples of tough questions:

- A team leader remarks to another member of the group: "The one-day promotion assumes it will not rain on June 5. What will you do if it rains?"
- The division general manager says to the manufacturing manager, "The delivery date you promised assumes that the one supplier you have for the main components will deliver as promised. Suppose they don't? Why do you depend so heavily on one supplier?"
- The vice president sends a memo to the sales manager: "I share your pride in the fact that sales are up 10 percent, but how does that compare to the sales increase of our three biggest competitors?"

To prepare yourself for answering tough questions, challenge your plan of action. Ask yourself: "What have I missed? What else should I have thought about? What could possibly go wrong with my plan?"

Advisor

Asking tough questions is cool. It adds immensely to your stature as a leader because many people expect a leader to ask provocative questions. Leaders are sometimes regarded not as people with the right answers, but as those with the right questions. Nevertheless, at times you may want to go beyond just asking tough questions. You may want to have some alternatives in mind that might have escaped the group members. However, do not jump right in and present your alternatives. Wait until people have responded to the tough questions. You then say, "Great, but have you also considered...?"

When?

Being good at asking tough questions requires developing the right mental habits. When reviewing the work or proposals of others, ask yourself these five questions:

1. Where's the hidden flaw in this?
2. How could this be better?
3. What didn't he, she, or they think of?
4. Where are the backup plans in case something goes wrong?
5. Nothing is this good; what would the CEO think of it?

Tough questions can be asked during group meetings, individual meetings, and while traveling with a work associate. But time the question for a moment when you think the other person would be receptive to heavy thinking. Avoid something like, "Please pass the ketchup. And by the way, do you think you should abolish the human resources department?"

Put Some Creative Punch into Your Thinking

Creativity gives you a tremendous edge as a leader. Developing a great idea or two enhances your credibility with your constituents. If you forage through the career path of top executives, you find that many key people launched their careers with a good idea. An outstanding example is Kim Polese, at one time a member of the Sun Microsystems team that developed Java. She is now the CEO of Marimba, a company that develops products to bring Internet information to people—the "push" strategy that brings information to you. You inform the system ahead of time that you are interested in information about the future. When such information occurs, it appears on your computer monitor, waiting for you. The information you need has been pushed through to your attention. In contrast, the "pull" strategy refers to pulling something up from a large database, such as using the key word "futurist" on an Internet search engine.

> **Another Perspective**
>
> Creativity can also be regarded as lateral thinking—a mental process that spreads out to find many different alternative solutions to a problem. For example, a human resources manager might ask, "How many different positions in this company can be performed by people whose welfare support will be discontinued?" Vertical thinking on the same topic would be, "What position do we have that could be filled by somebody coming off welfare?"

Polese's creative contribution was not so much in developing Java but in seeing its two enormous possibilities. First, it was not dependent on any existing platform. Second, Java could create lively Web pages in place of ordinary text. Instead of the World Wide Web being like radio, it could become like color TV.

Leaders think as Polese does. They see possibilities and opportunities others overlook. Instead of being locked into traditional ways of looking at objects and ideas, they think imaginatively. Here are seven key steps you can take to sharpen your creative problem-solving ability:

1. Keep track of your original ideas by maintaining an idea notebook or computer file. Few people have such uncluttered minds that they can recall all their past flashes of insight, especially when they need them.
2. Stay current in your field and hunt for ideas. Having current facts at hand gives you the raw material to link information creatively. Creativity often takes the form of associating ideas that were previously unassociated. An example is linking the idea of selling movie tickets with the idea of selling tickets through vending machines.
3. Participate in creative hobbies, such as doing puzzles and exercises or pursuing arts and crafts. Learning another language well (or not so well) also fosters innovation because you are forced to think in new and different ways.
4. Adopt a risk-taking attitude when you find creative solutions. You will inevitably fail a few times—not to worry. One or two innovative ideas per year is sufficient to develop a reputation as a creative problem-solver.
5. Develop a creative mental set. Allow your foolish side to emerge. Creativity requires a degree of intellectual playfulness and immaturity. Many creative people are accomplished practical jokers.
6. Be curious about your environment. The person who routinely questions how things work, or why they do not work, is often likely to have an idea for improvement.
7. Identify the time when you are most creative. Attempt to accomplish your creative work during that period. Many people are at their peak of creative productivity after ample rest, so work on your most vexing problem at the beginning of the workday.

Keep in mind an important point about creative problem solving. The more ideas you generate, the more likely you are to find a great idea. Creative problem solving is a numbers game.

Advisor

To become a creative problem-solver, you may have to overcome your belief in two myths. One myth is that people are either creative or not creative. In reality, creativity is like height and intelligence; everybody has it but in varying degrees. A second myth is that creativity applies only to the arts and technical fields. In truth, creativity is just as important in business as anywhere else.

Develop Your Insight

A distinguishing intellectual strength of leaders is that they can size up situations and people and arrive at an in-depth understanding that others might miss. This is the same ability that enables leaders to ask tough questions. A major advantage of a penetrating insight is that it helps another person understand a situation more clearly, spotting the illogic in their thinking. (The term *penetrating insight* is redundant because an insight penetrates. In fact, the French word for insight is *penetration*!) The other person you help often appreciates your efforts and is drawn to you because of your contribution.

Andrew Grove, the CEO of Intel, has been a well-known business leader for many years. Grove has an affinity for offering insight about business. His favorite motto (insight) is "Only the paranoid survive."

When you first hear this statement, you might think that Grove is paranoid. When you think about his motto, however, you realize that in a highly competitive industry such as computer chips, suspicion is a success strategy. For example, Grove has spent millions of dollars in legal fees to sue companies for alleged copyright and patent violations.

Developing powers of penetrating thinking requires intense listening and concentration. Search for incongruities and underlying meanings. Here are two examples to help you appreciate the nature of offering another person a breakthrough insight:

Alan's breakthrough insight: One of the people in Alan's group, who is 37 years old, says that he is too old to work on an MBA. He protests, "It would take me four years at night to earn an MBA. By then I will be 41 years old." Alan responds, "How old will you be in four years if you do not get an MBA?" The group member then suddenly realizes that time will pass regardless of whether he fills it with an important personal and professional accomplishment.

> **Another Perspective**
>
> Penetrating insights can enhance your leadership effectiveness in another way. You might discover aspects about yourself that could profit from improvement. A manger might ask himself, "Hmm, I've been downsized three times. Is there something I'm doing wrong that has put me on the hit list three times?"

Julie's breakthrough insight: One of Julie's peers says that she is terribly frustrated in her career because her previous three managers were too stupid to understand her contribution. She therefore has not been able to advance in responsibility. Julie responds, "Three stupid managers in a row seems implausible. Could it be that you are not packaging your ideas in a way that management can see the relevance of your work?" A light bulb flashes, and Julie's coworker begins to assess what she could possibly do better.

Offering penetrating insights to others enhances your leadership effectiveness because such insights sometimes help people overcome behavior that is blocking their progress. The right insight might help another person exit the path of self-defeating behavior.

How Do I Develop a Leader's Ability to Read People?

Another distinguishing characteristic of successful leaders is the ability to size up or read other people. They make rapid judgments about the capabilities and foibles of others. Many business leaders I have known have sharper insights into others than do specialists in human behavior.

Many leaders believe that their most important skill is their ability to read people. The ability shows up not only in hiring people but also in choosing the right people to handle an assignment and in choosing the right supplier.

Sharpening your ability to size up people follows many of the same suggestions provided earlier in the chapter for developing your intuition. You needs loads of study, practice, and feedback. Here are a few starter suggestions:

- Sigmund Freud believed that almost no behavior is random. Whatever a person says or does has meaning, and your job is to figure out what it means. For example, if a person is late twice for an appointment with you, it might indicate a lack of commitment to your cause or purpose.

- Make a few predictions about people you meet for the first time, record those predictions, and then see whether they prove to be true. For example, you might observe that a new vice president talks a lot during his first visit to your office. You jot down "compulsive talker, mild listening disorder." As time goes by, verify your hunch by speaking to others and making additional observations.
- While dining with people, check out the process they use to select from the menu. If a person asks a lot of questions and even encourages the server to make the choice, it could mean he or she is indecisive. Follow up your hunch about indecisiveness by seeing how that person handles decision-making in other situations. Make additional observations and attempt to verify them by noting the person's behavior in different surroundings.
- Observe how another person treats restaurant staff or store associates. Again, verify your observations by comparing the person's treatment of these people with how he or she treats people in other situations.
- Attempt to make predictions about people's behavior in general by the way they dress, maintain the interior of their cars, or organize their desks. Verify your hunch by comparing it to observed behavior in other situations. One hunch might be, "This person is too neat and structured to be creative."

> **Watch Out!**
> In the process of interpreting the behavior of other people, do not start to think that you are always right. For example, a cough during a meeting could mean that a person is bored or anxious. It could also mean the person has a sore throat.

The general point of these suggestions is that you can sharpen your insights into people by making guesses about their character or behavior. You then look for corroborating evidence in other circumstances. Bit by bit, your judgments will sharpen, and you will have honed another important leadership skill.

The Least You Need to Know

- Pay attention to your intuition.
- Becoming a big thinker is important for effective leadership.
- Ask tough questions.
- Use creative thinking to solve problems.
- Enhance your ability to read people.

Chapter 9

How About a More Charismatic You?

In This Chapter

- What charisma really means
- How to express your feelings assertively to contribute to your charisma
- Suggestions for being enthusiastic, optimistic, and energetic
- How to use candor as part of your charisma
- Suggestions for using animated facial expressions to enhance your charisma
- Suggestions for looking powerful and acting powerful

Sue and Rob were being considered for the general manager position at a division of a large clothing manufacturer. The company search committee submitted its final recommendations to the CEO. The committee said that both candidates were well qualified but that Rob had slightly stronger qualifications. "Why?" asked the CEO.

The head of the search committee indicated that Rob had a stronger technical background in textiles and was more experienced with finances.

In addition, he had a good track record of working with labor unions. The search committee also reported that Sue was well qualified, but she was not quite as strong as Rob in those three critical areas.

After pausing for a few seconds, the CEO said, "Thank you; I've made up my mind. Let's hire Sue. The slight edge Rob has in relevant business experience does not counterbalance Sue's charisma. Our big problem at this division is that the work force is uninspired. Rob is a strong candidate, but Sue's leadership qualities make her my first choice."

As this example indicates, being charismatic can often give you the edge in boosting your career. In this chapter, you will learn what charisma really means and how you can develop a sensible plan for developing your own charismatic qualities.

What in the World Is It? And How Can I Get It?

You have probably heard the word *charisma* hundreds of times in recent years. To be called charismatic is a strong compliment, and to be called noncharismatic is a mild insult. Many people who do not believe they are charismatic want to become charismatic. Yet they are discouraged because they do not believe that charisma is a quality that can be developed. In their minds, charisma is much like height. They think it is a good quality that cannot be learned!

Before I move on to the good news about charisma (that maybe you can learn it), first take a careful look at what it means. Although the term has at least 12 slightly different meanings, for our purposes, charisma is personal charm and magnetism that is used to lead others.

Despite the fact that charisma appears to be a deep-rooted personality characteristic, much of it can be learned. For example, being emotionally expressive is a major contributor to charisma—and you can learn to become more emotionally expressive. Keep in mind also that if you are already perceived by many people as charismatic, you can further develop your charismatic qualities.

> **Key Word**
> Here is another meaning to ponder: **Charisma** is a special quality of leaders whose purposes, powers, and extraordinary determination differentiate them from others.

One more important fact before you dig into how to recognize and acquire charisma: As I just hinted, charisma is a perception. Although you want people to perceive you as charismatic, you can never hit 100 percent. Even the most charismatic leaders are regarded as bland or even detestable by some. For example, when people are asked to name a charismatic business leader, the name Lee Iacocca still surfaces. People remember how Iacocca charmed the public, the federal government, and company employees into helping Chrysler Corporation rebound from near disaster.

Despite Iacocca's many fans, admirers, and followers, he turned off many people. He was accused of being racist (anti-Japanese), sexist, vulgar, crude, and manipulative. Furthermore, at least one biographer accused Iacocca of taking too much credit for the ideas of others.

With this proviso in mind that charisma is a subjective perception, check out the following examples of charismatic leaders from the world of business:

- **Larry Bossidy, the CEO of Allied Signal.** His tough talk and hard-hitting demeanor make his managers jump to reach the stretch targets he sets for them. Bossidy's charisma contributes to his status as one of the world's most in-demand executives for top leadership jobs at major corporations.
- **Oprah Winfrey, the CEO of Harpo Entertainment.** One of the world's best-known public figures, Winfrey charms millions of television viewers with her presence. The mention of a novel on her show turns it into a best-seller. Winfrey is also a warm, compassionate boss whose charisma and power create loyal disciples.
- **Herb Kelleher, the CEO of Southwest Airlines.** A combination of a stand-up comic, marketing genius, and inspiring business leader, Kelleher captivates customers and employees. His successful company is one of the most widely studied in business schools. Somehow his outrageous behavior (such as kissing male and female employees on the mouth and chain smoking) is tolerated and adored.
- **Michael Milken, now the head of his own investment firm and volunteer math teacher to underprivileged children.** In his former glory days, Milken was paid $500 million in one year. As the self-anointed king of junk bonds, he mesmerized thousands of finance professionals into believing he was the savior of small businesses. Even while serving time in jail for violating security laws, his loyal band of followers attested to his greatness. (Milken illustrates that charisma can be used to accomplish evil as well as good deeds.)

Working for a charismatic leader is somewhat like being married to or living with someone you find attractive and stimulating. He or she is fun to be around. Perhaps not every day is outrageously exciting, but the charismatic leader gives you an extra reason to come to work. You think the guy or gal is wonderful to be around, and you are willing to extend yourself to please him or her.

Learn to Express Your Feelings

The best recognized way to develop charisma is to learn to express your feelings more openly and freely. A starting point in learning to be more emotionally expressive is to gauge your present status on this key aspect of behavior. Take the following quiz to help you analyze your current level of emotional expressiveness.

Scoring and interpretation. Add the numbers you circled, and use the following as a guide to your level of emotionality with respect to being charismatic and dynamic:

90–100: Your level of emotionality could be interfering with your charisma. Many others interpret your behavior as out of control.

70–89: Your level of emotionality is about right for a charismatic individual. You are emotionally expressive, yet your level of emotional expression is not so intense as to be bothersome.

10–69: Your level of emotionality is probably too low to enhance your charisma. To become more charismatic and dynamic, you must work hard at expressing your feelings.

Now that you have given careful thought to your level of emotionality, you are in a position to judge how much development you need to become more emotionally expressive. People who want to improve their leadership effectiveness often need to enhance their emotional expressiveness. Of course, some people give free rein to their emotions. These folks might need to learn how to express feelings in a more constructive way to be truly charismatic. My suggestion that emotional expressiveness contributes to charisma may only work about 90 percent of the time. (Note: The principles of leadership are not as accurate as those for chemistry or physics.)

Connect Feelings with Facts

So you know you need to express your emotions more effectively. But do you know how you feel?

The Emotional Expressiveness Scale

Indicate how well each of the following statements describes you by circling the best answer: very inaccurately (VI); inaccurately (I); neutral (N); accurately (A); very accurately (VA).

	VI	I	N	A	VA
1. While watching a movie there are times when I will shout out in laughter or approval.	1	2	3	4	5
2. During a group meeting, I have occasionally shouted my approval with a statement such as "Yes" or "Fantastic."	1	2	3	4	5
3. During a group meeting, I have occasionally expressed disapproval by shouting an expression such as "absolutely not" or "horrible."	1	2	3	4	5
4. Several times, while attending a meeting, someone has said to me, "You look bored."	5	4	3	2	1
5. Several times while attending a social gathering, someone has said to me, "You look bored."	5	4	3	2	1
6. Many times while at social gatherings or business meetings, people have asked me, "Are you falling asleep?"	5	4	3	2	1
7. I thank people profusely when they do me a favor.	1	2	3	4	5
8. It's not unusual for me to cry at an event such as a wedding, graduation ceremony, or engagement party.	1	2	3	4	5
9. Reading about or watching sad news events, such as an airplane crash, brings tears to my eyes.	1	2	3	4	5
10. When I was younger, I got into more than my share of physical fights or shouting matches.	1	2	3	4	5
11. I dread having to express anger toward a coworker.	5	4	3	2	1
12. I have cried among friends more than once.	1	2	3	4	5
13. Other people have told me that I am affectionate.	1	2	3	4	5
14. Other people have told me that I am cold and distant.	5	4	3	2	1
15. I get so excited watching a sporting event that my voice is hoarse the next day.	1	2	3	4	5
16. It is difficult for me to express love toward another person.	5	4	3	2	1
17. Even when alone, I will sometimes shout in joy or anguish.	1	2	3	4	5
18. Many people have complimented me on my smile.	1	2	3	4	5
19. People who know me well can easily tell what I am feeling by the expression on my face.	1	2	3	4	5
20. More than once, people have said to me, "I don't know how to read you."	5	4	3	2	1
TOTAL					

Discover your emotional expressiveness.

In general, people do not have much trouble making facts known to other people. How you communicate those facts (your feelings and attitudes) may be creating a problem. For example, it is easier to say to a work associate, "You promised me your input by today," than to say, "I'm disappointed that you did not follow through on your commitment to give me your input by today." Maybe you shouldn't be disappointed, but these are your honest feelings. Effective leaders show their feelings.

Here is the hard part. To supplement your statements of fact, you must identify your feelings associated with the fact. The feeling points to an internal reaction you have to an object or person. Suppose you are applying new software to a work problem. After one hour of trying, the software does what you want it to do. The facts surrounding the event include ideas like these:

- "It took one hour for me to get the software to run right."
- "I stuck with the job and I was finally successful."
- "I worked my way through the task without asking a computer expert to help me."
- "I fell behind in my work because I spent so much time playing with the software."
- "I learned a new skill that will help me when I face a similar problem in the future."

Advisor

To supplement your statements of fact, you must identify your feelings associated with the fact. So doing will help you appear more emotionally expressive and charismatic. In spare moments, write down or think about events that have happened to you recently. Identify the facts, then specify the feeling associated with the facts. As you look through the rear view mirror of your car, you might note factually that a police officer on a motorcycle is approaching you rapidly and the motorcycle siren is screeching. Your associated feelings might be, "I'm humiliated, ticked off, and angry. If I get nailed for a speeding ticket, I'll be disgusted with myself."

All of the preceding factual statements reflect your intelligence and good problem-solving ability. However, they do not express your *feelings* surrounding the event. If you can identify your feelings in everyday events, you take a giant step toward becoming more emotionally expressive. Here are some of the feelings most likely associated with the preceding facts:

- "I'm so frustrated that it took me an hour to get the software to run right."
- "I'm elated. My persistence paid off. After sticking with the job, I was finally successful."
- "I'm so proud. I worked my way through the task without asking a computer expert to help me."
- "I'm so upset. I fell behind in my work because I spent so much time with the new software."
- "I'm excited. I learned a new skill that will help me when I face a similar problem in the future."

After developing skills in identifying your feelings, the next step is to practice expressing them to others. A general strategy is to reinforce many of the factual statements you make with the feelings behind them. To be perceived as dynamic, you must express your feelings to others as well as yourself. Here are a few examples of how charismatic people reinforce facts with feelings in speaking to others:

Editor to Editorial Assistant: "You put in ten hours of personal time to complete the project. It excites me that you care so much about the company."

Restaurateur to Executive Chef: "We cut our expenses without laying off people or sacrificing quality. I want to share my delight with you."

Where Do You Get Enthusiasm, Optimism, and Energy?

A remarkable quality of charismatic people is that they maintain high enthusiasm, optimism, and energy throughout their entire workday and beyond. An executive search consultant (a.k.a. headhunter) based in New York City made this comment about the strongest prospects he targets:

"I've had meetings as late as 10 at night with the executives I'm pursuing. They are as fresh as if it were 8:30 in the morning. You'll never hear one of them complain about how late it is or that he or she is exhausted. When these managers talk about their jobs or careers, they have a gleam in their eyes."

Becoming more energetic isn't as simple as tapping a toggle button. Elevating your energy—the main ingredient of charisma—takes considerable work. The following suggestions will get you started:

- Get ample rest at night and sneak in a 15-minute nap during the day when possible. If you have a dinner meeting where you want to shine, take a nap and a shower before the meeting.
- Switch to a healthy, energy-enhancing diet.
- Keep chopping away at your To Do list so you do not have unfinished tasks on your mind, draining your energy.
- Attempt to get your personal problems under control so they do not drain your productive energy from work. Similarly, get your work problems under control so they do not drain energy from your personal life.

Key Word
A person who has an **action orientation** is a person who wants to get things accomplished and decisions implemented.

Another aspect of being enthusiastic, optimistic, and energetic is maintaining an *action orientation*. "Let's do it!" is the battle cry of the charismatic person.

An action orientation also means that you prefer not to agonize over dozens of facts and nuances before making a decision. After enough information is collected to reinforce intuition, the charismatic person takes action and encourages other people to do the same.

Be Candid

The truth hurts, but this doesn't seem to deter charismatic leaders. They are remarkably candid and open with people. Although not overly insensitive, the charismatic leader is typically explicit in giving his or her assessment of a situation. A charismatic sales manager told one of her sales reps, "I know you want to become a sales manager, but I could not honestly recommend you for such a position now. You are too disorganized and impulsive." The sales rep was shocked and disappointed at first but learned an important lesson. He was jolted into realizing that how he performs today influences his opportunities for the future.

Charismatic people are candid on the positive as well as the negative side. They size up people and situations quickly and accurately and are willing to share those perceptions. Charismatic people speak directly rather than indirectly. As a result, other people know where they stand.

Expressing thoughts directly parallels expressing feelings directly. Instead of asking a group member, "Are you terribly busy this afternoon?" the charismatic leader asks, "I need your help this afternoon. Are you available?"

Advisor

Candor—on both the negative and positive side—is part of a charismatic person's tool kit. As long as you are not insensitive to the feelings of others, an open expression of your feelings and opinions has a magnetic pull. One reason candor is so effective is that it is distinctive. Only a minority of people are candid.

Becoming candid is not easy if you have a deep-rooted habit of talking in circles and softening your ideas. An important goal in expressing your candid thoughts and feelings is that the people with whom you interact should have no doubt about your true opinion.

Just before expressing your opinion about a person, idea, or object, prepare a ten-word statement in your mind. This activity will build your skill in expressing thoughts candidly. Practice it often. Here are six examples of candid expressions that you can use on the job:

1. You are definitely promotable.
2. Your job will be terminated in 30 days.
3. You are an outstanding performer.
4. One reason I want you on our team is because of your honesty.
5. One reason I don't want you on our team is that you have a reputation for being devious.

6. Sorry, I will not be placing another order with your firm. We have chosen another supplier who has higher-quality products.

If you are just learning to be candid, the initial results are likely to be a pleasant surprise. Quite often the recipient of the candid expression will say something to this effect, "Thanks for being honest. I'm glad I know where I stand."

A charismatic leader's success with being candid is partially attributable to the way in which the message is delivered. A negative message is most likely to be accepted when it is delivered in a matter-of-fact, nonjudgmental manner. The message should also be nonhostile and nonretaliatory.

Another important part of a charismatic leader's candor is that he or she formulates a believable vision. For example, an automotive plant manager might state, "We will become the plant with the highest quality and lowest accident rate in North America."

Use Animated Facial Expressions

A person who resembles a statue is rarely described as charismatic. To exhibit personal dynamism, it is essential to frequently use animated facial expressions. Use big smiles, little smiles, expressions of delight, frowns, scowls, looks of puzzlement, surprise, and reassuring nods. Visualize any leader whom you regard as charismatic. My guess is that this man or woman uses a variety of facial expressions in the presence of others.

To develop your skill at using animated facial expressions, follow these suggestions:

- Pay attention to leaders you admire and note their facial expressions. Practice modeling their behavior.
- Practice in front of a mirror or camcorder. Videotaping is better than using a mirror because many people find it difficult to modify their facial expressions when looking into a mirror.
- While looking into the mirror or recording on tape, think of various moods you want to project. Then do your best to match your facial expression to the mood.
- If you need some guidelines for matching facial expressions to your moods, emulate television actors, newscasters, newsmakers, and especially comedians.

Remember that animated facial expressions project leadership characteristics. They reflect the fact that you are listening and involved in the activities of the moment.

> **Another Perspective**
>
> 
>
>
> Experts don't agree on why some people are perceived as charismatic. The generally accepted idea is that an individual's personal characteristics create the impression of charisma. Another viewpoint is that if a leader accomplishes great results (such as Lew Gerstner's triumphs at IBM), he or she is perceived as charismatic. In other words, results lead to charisma rather than charisma leading to results.

Do You Look Powerful? Do You Act Powerful?

An indispensable part of projecting charisma is to look and act powerful. Looking powerful is more subtle than it appears on the surface. If you take literally the advice of wardrobe consultants, you will look like a sales associate in a retail store or a young professional in most metropolitan offices.

On the other hand, if you ignore conventional wisdom about looking powerful, you risk looking unimportant and lacking in charisma. Here are some specific ways to increase your power look:

- Dress with taste and style. Suits for men and women should be conservative but not overly conservative. Your shirts may have initialed cuffs. Consider using an expensive fountain pen and watch. Women may consider adding a scarf to their outfits. If casual clothing is the norm, wear carefully pressed pants or slacks, starched, open-collar, button-down shirts, and a sport coat.
- Decorate your office or cubicle tastefully, perhaps with stainless steel, leather, and polished glass. Use family photos and other mementos sparingly.
- On occasion, when standing, place your hands on your hips and place your feet shoulder-width apart. (Try it; it projects self-confidence.)
- For emphasis when speaking, point the index finger parallel to the ground and the thumb at a right angle—similar to aiming a water pistol. (Do this only if you feel comfortable with this gesture.)

Do You Move and Act Purposefully?

People who stride though the workplace as if they have an urgent intent project charisma and personal dynamism. Top-level managers move and act purposefully even when they are passing through a lobby. Keep these examples in mind:

At meetings. You arrive early for a meeting. Don't stand outside the room waiting for others—it makes you look as if you're wasting time. Instead, take a seat in the meeting room and either read your memos or work on your To Do list.

In the hallway. You are walking down the hallway to attend a meeting. Stop to chat only if it meets some business purpose. Otherwise, walk in a straight line at a brisk pace. Charismatic people are not rudderless.

The Least You Need to Know

- Charisma is almost universally recognized as a major leadership quality.
- Although some successful leaders are not *universally* perceived as charismatic by many people, attempting to lead others without charisma puts you at a disadvantage.
- Although popular opinion suggests that charisma is a mysterious inner quality possessed by a small number of captivating people, you can develop many of the qualities associated with charisma.
- The most effective and feasible methods of developing or enhancing your charisma include learning to express your feelings more assertively and becoming more enthusiastic, optimistic, and energetic.

Chapter 10

Communicate Like a Leader

In This Chapter

- Embellishing what you say to add impact
- Using metaphors and analogies to inspire others
- Telling a story
- The message your body language sends
- Projecting power with your linguistic style
- Junk words, clichés, and other detractors

The CEO of a company that makes interiors for corporate jets was touring its largest manufacturing site. Stopping by the department that installs seating, he asked the supervisor, Herb, how well his department was meeting its goals. Herb replied:

"Like, I'm not sure. We have lots of goals, you know. Like it's tough figuring out what you guys really want. You know, it's crazy down here. You know where I'm coming from?"

The CEO wasn't exactly sure where Herb was coming from—but he was sure where Herb wasn't going. The CEO told the plant manager that Herb was not to be promoted. In addition, the CEO requested that the plant manager carefully review Herb's performance to make sure he was an effective leader.

Maybe you feel sorry for Herb and believe that the CEO judged him too harshly based on a brief interaction. Yet an inescapable fact is that to be credible as a leader, you must communicate as a leader does. In this chapter, you will learn about the major distinguishing feature of the communication styles of leaders. Obviously not all effective leaders communicate in the same manner, but important similarities are worth your careful study.

Impress Them with Heavy-Impact Language

Certain words used in the proper context give power and force to your speech. Used naturally and sincerely, these words can strengthen your leadership stature and your ability to inspire others. Current buzzwords usually have a positive impact. Note the emphasis on *current.* Yesterday's buzzwords have low impact. Here is a sampling of heavy-impact, embellishing language:

- Tell group members that you want them to "unleash their creative potential" instead of simply asking for a few suggestions.
- Explain that your group has a "well-articulated vision of where we are headed," instead of simply saying that you prepared a list of goals.
- Talk about having attended a "prestigious" trade show rather than simply a trade show.
- Use the expression "on the verge" of accomplishing something as long as a project is underway.
- Mention that you want to "bond" with customers instead of simply stating that you want to establish a good working relationship.

> CAUTION
>
> **Watch Out!**
> Using heavy-impact, embellishing language is an important addition to your leadership tool kit. If embellishment is taken too far, too often, the embellisher might appear deceptive and devious.

- Ask the team to "do it right the first time" instead of simply avoiding mistakes.
- When your group picks up some useful feedback from a customer satisfaction survey, proclaim that your unit "demonstrated the capabilities of a learning organization."
- When your department wins an interdepartmental skirmish or wins a bid over a competitor, say that you "nuked" them.

Dazzle with Analogies and Metaphors

A well-chosen analogy or metaphor appeals to your intellect and imagination. Effective leaders therefore make frequent use of analogies and metaphors. An analogy draws attention to the similarity between the features of two things so people can make a comparison. "Our company is much like Microsoft in its early days," is an analogy many founders of small high-tech companies make when attempting to inspire workers.

A metaphor is also a comparison, but it is less obvious than an analogy. The comparison is between two objects not ordinarily associated with each other. Comparing a small high-tech company to a cougar cub is a metaphor. Whether your comparison is a metaphor or analogy is not important. What really counts is whether the comparison grabs people. Workers are inspired by analogies and metaphors that are relevant to the challenges they face. Here is a sampling of analogies and metaphors leaders have used in their interactions with group members:

- Up to now, our group has been playing roller derby. It's time we started acting as a football team.
- We are a young company, competing against the established giants, much like Compaq Computer 23 years ago.
- Let's hang in there and pull together. I envision a great success for our delivery service. Don't forget that Federal Express started from scratch in 1975 and now has 110,000 employees worldwide.

> **Watch Out!**
> Analogies and metaphors can be potent motivational tools. However, they can also fall flat and annoy people. Before using your metaphor or analogy on the job, first try it out with a friend or family member. Carefully watch the expression on his or her face to see if it works. Also get the other person's opinion in words.

- Don't be discouraged by placing second in our bid to receive that contract. Michael Jordan didn't make his high-school basketball team on the first try.
- I like to think of our team as a group of wallabies, those lovable kangaroo-like animals from Australia. Most people like us, but we would be better off if we weren't hopping in so many directions.
- Don't let those comments about our new model being mundane discourage you. Look at the bum rap people give donkeys, yet donkey-owners love their hard-working, faithful animals. A donkey can be counted on for years of good performance. Besides that, a donkey-owner forms an emotional attachment to his or her unglamorous sidekick.

Are you looking for a useful analogy or metaphor? A good starting point is to make comparisons with sports, successful companies, the military, and animals. Sexual analogies can inspire some people, but others perceive them as a form of sexual harassment.

Inspire with Story-Telling

Another aspect of the communication style of effective leaders is that they make extensive use of memorable anecdotes to get messages across. They inspire and instruct team members by telling fascinating stories, thus managing by anecdote. Using anecdotes is a powerful leadership technique for several reasons:

- People like to hear anecdotes.
- Anecdotes help build the corporate culture.
- Workers can remember a principle or policy better if it is accompanied by an anecdote.

Message-sending anecdotes might relate to such subjects as a company president who goes out of his or her way to help an individual customer or a lower-ranking employee who defied authority to meet his or her responsibilities. For example, a receptionist at IBM denied admission to the company chairman, Tom Watson, because Watson was not wearing a security badge. Instead of firing the young woman, Watson praised her devotion to duty.

An inspiring anecdote supports an important company value such as customer satisfaction, quality, or employee safety. At Saks Fifth Avenue, for example, many employees have heard the story of how far management will go to satisfy a customer. The scenario occurred at the original Saks on Fifth Avenue in Manhattan. According to the legend, an elderly customer insisted that the only dress she wanted in the store was the one in the window. A store manager overheard the conversation between the store associate and the customer. The store manager removed the dress from the mannequin to satisfy the customer and placed another dress on the mannequin. The customer was delighted, and the store associate was shocked because window displays were considered sacrosanct.

Advisor

Telling anecdotes is such a useful management and leadership technique that it merits special attention. Create a useful anecdote file of your own. Collect anecdotes you observe personally, those you hear from others, and those you read in books, magazines, and newsletters. You might even find a useful anecdote on the Internet. As part of developing your anecdotal skills, observe how people being interviewed on talk shows present anecdotes. Another potential model is a professional storyteller. Perhaps you will have a chance to observe one. Also, observe comedians at comedy clubs and on TV. They often use anecdotes as a form of humor.

Does Your Nonverbal Language Project Leadership?

You're probably familiar with the different ways of communicating nonverbally, through gestures, posture, and eye movements. Nonverbal communication is the transmission of messages through means other than words. It includes body language as well as such diverse behavior as appearance, tone of voice, and the surroundings in which you deliver a message.

Certain gestures signal others that you are self-confident and a leader. Not everybody interprets body language and other nonverbal signals uniformly. Using the types of nonverbal communication described here will impress many, although not all, of the people you want to influence and inspire.

Another Perspective
A contrary point of view is to avoid using some forms of nonverbal behavior because they can have different meanings in different cultures. In the United States and Canada, "perfect" is symbolized by joining your thumb and forefinger to make a circle. According to Letitia Baldrige, in Japan this gesture means you are expecting a kickback. In France it means "zero," and in many other countries the same symbol is an outright vulgarity.

Key Word
Congruence is a way of synchronizing the ways in which you attempt to deliver a message. If you want people to clean up their work areas, send the information in a neat form—not a messy-looking e-mail message or written note. And when you express sympathy, make a conscious effort to look sad, and have a sorry-sounding tone.

Get Your Verbal and Nonverbal Behavior in Synch

This section delves into specific aspects of nonverbal behavior that will strengthen your leadership ability. However, I first want you to be aware of the principle of *congruence*. Suppose you say to a group member, "I'm sorry to hear that your data file crashed. Tell me about it." At the same time, you have a concerned, saddened look on your face, and you squint intently. You sit in your chair as if you want to be there until the person finishes his or her story. You achieve congruence, and you come across as sympathetic—an important leadership characteristic.

Replay the same scenario. You make the statement, "I'm so sorry to hear that your data file crashed. Tell me about it." At the same time, you have a bored, disinterested look on your face. You shift your gaze in several directions. You fidget in your chair, and your posture appears aimed at leaving the scene quickly. You are displaying incongruence, and you leave the other person feeling flat and disappointed. Furthermore, you do not strengthen the relationship between you and the group member.

The important general principle is that you can strengthen your verbal message by ensuring that your words and nonverbal language are in synch. When your verbal and nonverbal messages match, you convey the impression that you are trustworthy and honest. If your nonverbal message reinforces your statement of concern, group members believe that you are interested in their plight.

Recognizing the importance of congruence in your communication is an important first step in becoming more congruent. Your aim is to integrate the various ways you send messages so that you appear more credible and influence others more effectively. Following are several actions that will help you become more congruent. Assuming this behavior will multiply the effectiveness of your communication:

- When you tell others you feel relaxed and happy or describe another positive state, consciously relax your muscles and facial expression.
- When you say to another person, "Tell me about your day (or vacation, new project, child, grandchild, spouse, significant other, or motorcycle)," gaze intently at the person and widen your eyes. Leaning toward the person also supports your request, as does a quizzical, inquiring look.
- When you deliver an affirmation to another person such as "We must have lunch" or "I'll call you," elevate or modulate your voice tone. Also, give at least a small smile and avoid a deadpan expression.

The focus now shifts to how various types of specific nonverbal communication can contribute to your effectiveness as a leader.

The Eyes Have It

When used congruently, the head, face, and eyes provide the clearest indication of attitude toward others. If you are addressing Carl, a group member, turn your head toward him, look at his face, and make eye contact. Your full attention suggests self-confidence and respect for Carl.

When you have good eye contact with the person you are addressing, that individual interprets what you have to say more favorably than if you avoid eye contact. If you make eye contact with group members in turn, they pay more attention to your message and perceive you as more confident.

Stand Up Straight!

Posture is perhaps the most obvious nonverbal signal of self-confidence and belief in yourself. Standing up straight generally reflects high self-confidence, whereas stooping and slouching indicate a poor self-image

> **Another Perspective**
> To strengthen your perception of the importance of good posture in creating a leadership image, visualize one or two of the political figures you admire the most. What is his or her posture like, even while seated? Or think of an outstanding sports leader (such as a coach). Carefully observe that individual's posture.

and weak leadership capability. Leaning toward other individuals suggests that you are favorably disposed toward them and what they have to say.

Personal Space

How far away do you stand from people you are attempting to influence? The distance can shape their perceptions of your effectiveness as a leader. If you are in actual physical contact with another person or up to 18 inches away, your message might be interpreted as a confidence or you might appear brash. However, you might also be perceived as intimidating or harassing.

Standing from one and one-half to four feet from the person you're addressing is best for projecting face-to-face leadership. If you move from four to eight feet away from the person you're addressing, you might appear to be shying away from others.

Watch Your Hands!

Hand gestures provide an opportunity to project confidence and an in-charge attitude. Consider these possibilities:

- Punch a fist into the air to mean "Let's do it!"
- Use a finger as a pointing rod to emphasize a point or to direct others.
- Use open-palm slapping of another's hand to signify strong agreement or to offer congratulations.
- Extending both palms in the same motion required for pushing a heavy object communicates forcefully the message, "I don't want to hear any more of this."

- Extend a thumb upward indicating strong approval.
- The politician-like two arms raised in a V-shape with the first two fingers of each hand also in a V-shape is a high-power leadership gesture of unity and victory.

How Do You Sound?

People often attach more significance to the way you say something than to what you say. A forceful voice, which includes a consistent tone without vocalized pauses, suggests power, control, and confidence. A whispery, wimpy voice detracts from a confident and take-charge image. A voice coach surveyed 1,000 men and women and asked, "Which irritating or unpleasant voice annoys you the most?" The answer was a whining, complaining, or nagging tone. To improve your voice quality, try these techniques:

- Listen to your recorded voice. Keep repeating the same message until you are satisfied that you sound like a confident person.
- Several times per week, visualize yourself speaking to group members. Practice using the voice quality you think conveys confident leadership.

Your Time Is Important

A subtle form of nonverbal communication in the workplace is how you use your time. Guarding time as a precious resource helps you project self-confidence and leadership. A statement such as, "I can give 15 minutes to your problem this Thursday at 3:45 p.m." says to another that you are in control of yourself. Too many of these statements, however, might make you appear unapproachable and lacking consideration.

Be prompt for meetings and, if you are the leader, start and stop meetings on time. Jot down appointments in your day planner or electronic device in front of others. Make references to dates one year into the future and beyond, such as "By 2002, we should have a 40 percent market share."

Advisor

Suppose you've tried several specific nonverbal communication signals on one or two people, and you don't get the response you wanted. Keep trying. Recognize that a given nonverbal signal (such as punching your fist into the air) influences some people but not others. Combine a few nonverbal signals, such as moving toward the person and using effective hand gestures.

Sometimes observing what nonverbal signals the other person uses will help you influence that person. For example, if your influence target likes to gently punch the arm of another person for emphasis, maybe you can get through to that person by tapping his or her arm.

Do You Appear Confident, Friendly, and Approachable?

Another important use of body language is presenting a confident but friendly image in the workplace. Such behavior is typical of the team, or participative, style of leader. Consider these nonverbal actions to indicate you are confident, friendly, and approachable:

- A loosened tie *and* slightly exposed throat can portray openness and informality (for men).
- Dominant people tend to stand with their toes pointing outward, whereas less dominant people point their toes slightly inward.
- Shrugged or rounded shoulders make you appear less threatening. Taking off a jacket with padded shoulders can make you appear less distant.
- Placing your forearms on the table, palms up, makes your words seem more sincere.
- Matching your body movements to those of the person you are communicating with (called *mirroring*) without being too obvious, creates a sense of solidarity that conveys a feeling of agreement with the other person.

The quickest way to improve your nonverbal communication is to relax. Take a deep breath and consciously allow your muscles to loosen. A relaxed person makes it easier for other people to relax, and you appear more confident and calm.

> **Key Word**
> **Mirroring** is copying the behavior of another person. For example, if the person you're talking with folds her arms, you fold yours as well. If the person crosses her legs, then you do it too. Mirroring subtly tells others that you want to have rapport with them.

Hit 'Em with Your Power-Oriented Language Style

A major part of persuading others and communicating as a leader involves choosing the right language style. I've already mentioned several aspects of language, or *linguistic style.* Although what makes a person persuasive is not entirely certain, several components of language style generally give power and authority to the message sender. Many of the following suggestions are based on the long-term research of linguist Deborah Tannen:

- Downplay uncertainty. If you are not confident of your opinion or prediction, make a positive statement anyway, such as saying, "I know this new system will cure our inventory problems."
- Use the pronoun "I" to receive more credit for your ideas. (Of course, this could backfire in a team-based organization.)
- Apologize infrequently, and particularly minimize saying, "I'm sorry."
- Offer negative feedback directly, rather than soften the feedback by first giving praise and then moving to the areas of criticism.
- Emphasize direct rather than indirect talk, such as saying, "I need your report by noon tomorrow" rather than "I'm wondering if your report will be available by noon tomorrow."

> **Key Word**
> A **linguistic style** is a person's characteristic speaking pattern. It involves such aspects of speech as amount of directness, pacing and pausing, word choice, and the use of communication devices such as jokes, figures of speech, anecdotes, questions, and apologies.

Using colorful, powerful words and a power-oriented communication style enhances the perception by others that you are a leader.

Junk Words and Pauses

Do you use any of these junk words or vocalized pauses?

- Like (used invariably before almost any expression).
- You know (to start almost any sentence and as a break within a sentence).
- You know what I'm saying?
- He goes (to mean he says).
- Uhhhhh.
- Tatatatatatata (a low, breathy whistle used continuously while searching for information, especially over the telephone).
- Frequent clearing of the throat for no physical reason.

An effective way to decrease the use of these extraneous words and nonwords is to tape your side of a phone conversation and then play it back. Once you hear how these junk words and vocalized pauses detract from your speech effectiveness, you begin to monitor your own speech patterns.

Hackneyed Clichés and Recycled Anecdotes

Clichés and familiar anecdotes can be helpful communication tools because they signify shared knowledge. Nevertheless, effective leaders use them sparingly. Here are a few overused expressions and anecdotes (if you've heard them once you've heard them a hundred times; okay, don't use that expression, either):

- Making an illogical, amusing statement (such as "Let's carefully plan what we did wrong last year") and then attributing it to Yogi Berra.
- "It's not over until the fat lady sings."
- "You can't make an omelet without breaking eggs."
- Telling people that Babe Ruth broke the record for home runs but that he also broke the record for strikeouts.
- To illustrate cross-cultural sensitivity, telling people the story about how Chevrolet ran into trouble marketing the Nova in Mexico because "nova" is a Spanish expression for "does not go."

- To illustrate serendipity, telling people the story about how Post-it notes were invented at 3M.

The problem with using threadbare clichés and anecdotes is that it makes you appear unimaginative, uninspired, and boring if the listener has heard the same thing several times before.

Does Every Noun Want to Be a Verb?

A while back in the business and government arenas, people started converting everyday nouns into verbs. The practice made sense. The pencil led people to say, "I'll pencil my comments directly on your memo," and the telephone became the basis for expressions such as "I'll telephone you tomorrow." Soon people were *photocopying, faxing,* and *e-mailing* each other. By 1996, in honor of the turnaround manager Al Dunlap, a company that was dramatically shrunk in size to reduce costs was said to have been *Dunlapped.*

As a leader, you want to appear current, so it makes sense to go along somewhat with the movement toward nouning. However, too much nouning makes you sound bureaucratic, immature, and verbally challenged. Top executives convert far fewer nouns into verbs than do workers at lower levels. Perhaps you've gone too far when you regularly incorporate phrases such as the following into your language:

> **Key Word**
> Although **nouning** is a common practice, these new verbs cannot be found in any dictionary. For example, does your dictionary have this verb—"anecdote your speeches"?

- Cell-phone me your response by noon.
- Red-mark anything you don't like in my report.
- Network the best people you know.
- TQM (or ISO 9000) our customer service department.
- Be careful not to Dilbert your employees.

The Least You Need to Know

- To influence others, use heavy-impact, embellishing language.
- Metaphors, analogies, and anecdotes can be powerful tools for inspiring group members.
- The skillful use of nonverbal communication is a key part of communicating.
- A comprehensive approach to communicating like a leader is to use a power-oriented language style.
- To help project a leadership image, avoid detractors such as junk words, vocalized pauses, insipid clichés, threadbare anecdotes, and turning too many nouns into verbs.

Chapter 11

How to Develop Credibility

In This Chapter

- Acting credible in an incredible world
- Developing your own ethical code
- A six-step guide to making ethical decisions
- Developing consistency between words and deeds
- How to look trustworthy

Jason is the owner of a rapidly growing cleaning service for offices, stores, and malls in north Florida. One Saturday morning, Jason was reviewing the company books. He noticed that one customer, a professional and medical building in Jacksonville, appeared to have double-paid one month's invoice. Monday morning, Jason stopped by the cubicle of company bookkeeper Nancy to discuss the situation.

Jason asked Nancy to investigate the apparent overpayment as soon as possible. Nancy followed through within an hour. She reported back to Jason at noon: "According to the customer's records, they did not pay double. Let's just keep the money as a little bonus. I bet we've underbilled many other customers."

"Absolutely not," said Jason. "Let's get to the bottom of the problem. I don't want to fight with a good customer about overpayment, but we must straighten out the account."

"Why all the fuss?" asked Nancy. "This is an overpayment, not an underpayment." Nancy finally straightened out the situation in the customer's favor. She thought about the incident for a few days, and then told her boss:

"Jason, that little incident with the customer who overpaid us helped me understand something important about you. I now know why the business is growing rapidly and our turnover is so low. Everybody trusts you."

Even if you are already honest and trustworthy, reading this chapter will help you enhance your leadership effectiveness. You will learn more about how trust enters into leadership and how to communicate trust to others. You will learn that projecting trust requires more than saying to group members, "I am not a crook."

Act Credible in an Incredible World

A few years ago, the American Management Association asked a panel of academics and other experts to describe the perfect leader for the '90s business world. Integrity and trustworthiness were the two qualities at the top of the list that were considered essential for leadership.

Integrity centers around values. Leaders with integrity are strongly dedicated to doing what they know is right. A small example is Jason, who took the initiative to credit a customer for an overpayment. A bigger example is the reputation for *integrity* that Hewlett-Packard leadership has developed. Top management insists on never releasing a product with known deficiencies. This does not mean every Hewlett-Packard product is perfect. It does mean, however, that company leaders do not intentionally look the other way when defective products are shipped to customers.

> **Key Word**
> **Integrity** is an unswerving adherence to moral and ethical principles. A person with high integrity is seen as honorable.

Studies have repeatedly demonstrated the common sense belief that people want leaders they can trust. Similarly, they want leaders who trust them. Integrity feeds trustworthiness because a leader with high integrity is trusted. Trust of business leaders has declined in recent years for several reasons:

- The disparity between compensation for top managers and compensation for workers has been increasing steadily. In 1996, for example, the average big company CEO received a 54 percent raise, whereas workers in general received a three percent increase. The average compensation of the same executives was 209 times that of a production worker.
- Many companies have continued to elevate executive pay while downsizing and cutting costs in other ways.
- Many employee pension funds have been depleted or eliminated despite legislation designed to protect pension funds. Large numbers of employees have been forced to retire without the benefit of a company pension to which they contributed for many years.
- Several well-known companies have been accused of exploiting child labor at overseas affiliates. Executives at these same companies are among the most elaborately paid and most celebrated as outstanding leaders.
- Top leaders at a few well-known companies have been accused of elaborate schemes of sexual harassment.

That's enough lecturing about morality and ethics for now. The following self-quiz gives you something concrete for assessing your ethical beliefs.

Scoring and interpretation: Add the numbers you circled to obtain your total score.

90–100: You are a strongly ethical person who may take a little ribbing from coworkers for being too straitlaced.

60–89: You show an average degree of ethical awareness and therefore should become more sensitive to ethical issues.

41–59: Your ethics are underdeveloped, but you at least have some awareness about ethical issues.

20–40: Your ethics are far below contemporary standards in business. Begin a serious study of business ethics.

The Ethical Reasoning Inventory

Describe how well you agree with each of the following statements. Use the following scale: Disagree strongly (DS); Disagree (D); Neutral (N); Agree (A); Agree strongly (AS).

	DS	D	N	A	AS
1. When applying for a job, I would cover up the fact that I had been fired from my most recent job.	5	4	3	2	1
2. Cheating just a few dollars in one's favor on an expense account is OK if a person needs the money.	5	4	3	2	1
3. Employees should inform on each other for wrongdoing.	1	2	3	4	5
4. It is acceptable to give approximate figures for expense account items when one does not have all the receipts.	5	4	3	2	1
5. I see no problem with conducting a little personal business on company time.	5	4	3	2	1
6. Just to make a sale, I would stretch the truth about a delivery date.	5	4	3	2	1
7. I would fix up a purchase order with a date just to close a sale.	5	4	3	2	1
8. I would flirt with my boss just to get a bigger salary increase.	5	4	3	2	1
9. If I received $300 for a one-time consulting job, I would report it on my income tax return.	1	2	3	4	5
10. I see no harm in taking home a few office supplies.	5	4	3	2	1
11. It is acceptable to read the e-mail messages and faxes of other workers, even when not invited to do so.	5	4	3	2	1
12. It is unacceptable to call in sick in order to take a day off, even if only done once or twice a year.	1	2	3	4	5
13. I would accept a permanent, full-time job even if I knew I wanted the job for only six months.	5	4	3	2	1
14. I would first check company policy before accepting an expensive gift from a supplier.	1	2	3	4	5
15. To be successful in business, a person usually has to ignore ethics.	5	4	3	2	1
16. If I felt physically attracted toward a job candidate I would hire that person over a more qualified candidate.	5	4	3	2	1
17. On the job, I tell the truth all the time.	1	2	3	4	5
18. Software should never be copied, except as authorized by the publisher.	1	2	3	4	5
19. I would authorize accepting an office machine on a 30-day trial period, even if I knew we had no intention of buying it.	5	4	3	2	1
20. I would never accept credit for a coworker's ideas.	1	2	3	4	5
TOTAL					

Check your ethical reasoning.

Advisor

Developing your sense of ethics helps you become more credible. A display of good ethics demonstrates that you are credible and honest. Given that ethical behavior is expected in almost all daily activities, it is necessary to behave ethically in a situation in which many others would act unethically. The study about Jason who returned an overpayment illustrates a display of good ethics. Another example would be to return a set of Super Bowl or major concert tickets to a vendor because you did not want your objectivity to be clouded.

Write Down What You Stand For

Given that most people want their leaders to be ethical, it is important to take constructive steps to be thoroughly ethical. Even if you have not been accused of being unethical, it still pays to ensure that you appear highly ethical to others. If others think you have a problem with ethical behavior, it could prevent you from obtaining a leadership position you desire or from being fully effective as a leader. A dynamic first step in elevating the ethical aura you create is to develop a *personal ethical code*. Write down what you consider to be right and wrong, good and bad, and ethical and unethical in the conduct of your job and career.

Key Word
Your **personal ethical code** should not be filed and forgotten. Refer to it periodically to make sure you are following your moral compass.

An ethical code determines what is right or wrong (or good or bad) based on values. You can find some hints for writing your ethical code by researching ethical codes developed for your company, industry, or profession. You might find a code of conduct in the company policy manual. Ask the receptionist in the office of your lawyer, physician, insurance representative, or investment broker for a copy of that field's ethical code. Yes, all of the preceding professions have written ethical codes. Company codes of ethics typically include entries such as the following:

- Comply with safety, health, and security regulations.
- Demonstrate courtesy, respect, honesty, and fairness.
- Exhibit good attendance and punctuality.
- Do not use abusive language.
- Do not offer bribes.
- Maintain confidentiality of records.
- Comply with accounting rules and controls.
- Do not use company property for personal benefit.
- Do not propagate false or misleading information.
- Do not sexually harass subordinates, coworkers, superiors, suppliers, or customers.
- Make decisions without regard for personal gain.
- Provide products and services of highest quality.

After you study a professional or company code of conduct, you might incorporate some of the ideas into your personal code of professional ethics. Also include in your personal code how far you will bend your rules in order to get ahead. Specify what is off-limits to you. Are you willing to take credit for the ideas of others? Back-stab? Laugh at jokes that you do not think are funny to please a key person?

Most people with a sense of common decency already know that such acts as accepting bribes, lying, and sexually harassing others are wrong. A code of ethics helps solidify your thinking and enables you to become a solid corporate citizen. As a result, your leadership stature will increase.

Advisor

Update your code as new workplace issues surface that involve ethics. For example, what about the ethics of putting stolen ideas or misleading information on your Web site? A new entry to your personal code might state, "I will not slam the competition on our Web site." Remember that your personal ethical code reflects your beliefs and values and is not necessarily based on the code of conduct used by your profession (such as accountants, purchasing agents, or engineers).

Jiffy Guide for Making Decisions in the Gray Zone

Many decisions are easy to evaluate with respect to ethics because they are obviously ethical or unethical. Tops Friendly Market, a large chain of supermarkets, recently decided to allocate one space in each store parking lot for expectant mothers. The sign is adorned with a stork. No need to ponder over the ethics of this decision. (Of course, women who are one or two month's pregnant face the ethical challenge of whether to hog the parking place.) At the unethical end of the continuum, there's also no need to ponder whether promoting friends of a family-owned business over more qualified candidates is ethical.

Ethical tests have been developed to help workers make choices about decisions in the gray zone—neither clearly right or wrong. Of course, what is in the gray zone depends on your values. Assume as a leader-manager you have decided that your exempt (from over-time regulations) employees should work Saturday mornings. A challenge you face is that the company has been downsized and it is deliberately understaffed.

You are contemplating using an interesting "motivator." You plan to casually mention to your staff that a large number of people in the labor market want their jobs. In other words, "If you don't like working Saturday mornings without extra pay, you can easily be replaced." You can run the contemplated decision through an ethical screen developed by the Center for Business Ethics at Bentley College. Ask yourself the following questions:

1. **Is it right?** The question is based on the theory of ethics that there are certain universally accepted guiding principles of right and wrong, such as "Thou shall not take false credit for the ideas of others," or "Thou shall not play video games during working hours." Some people think that the implied threat of firing violates the guiding principle of "Thou shall not manipulate people with too much force."
2. **Is it fair?** This question is based on the theory of justice implying that certain actions are just and other actions are unjust. Maybe it isn't fair to expect professionals to work every Saturday morning under the thinly veiled threat of being fired if they don't like it. Maybe, because the practice is not infrequent, it is fair. Remember, it's your call.
3. **Who gets hurt?** This question is based on the notion of attempting to do the greatest good for the greatest number of people. Some

people might say, "A lot of families will be hurt if a key family member has to work most Saturday mornings." Others might say, "If the exempt staff pulls together to increase company productivity, the company will be able to protect a lot of jobs."

4. **Would you be comfortable if the details of your decision were reported on the front page of your local newspaper or through your company's e-mail system?** Would you mind seeing the headline, "__________ orders professional staff to work Saturdays, under hint of being replaced"? Think it through.
5. **Would you tell your child (or a young relative) to do it?** Visualize telling a six-year old child, "I've got a great way of getting people to work on Saturday morning for no extra money. Let me tell you about it so you can do it in case you're the boss someday."
6. **How does it smell?** This question is based on a person's intuition and common sense. Some people might say, "My plan smells rotten. What a way to treat people." Others might say, "It smells fine. A professional person does what it takes to get the job done."

Excuse My Cliché, but Walk the Talk

A major workplace issue today is whether employees trust their leaders and managers. In the long run, group members who trust their leaders are likely to be more satisfied and perform better. The number one factor in gaining the trust of group members is to show consistency between intentions and actions.

"Walking the talk" means consistency between words and deeds. Suppose a CEO says, "Don't worry; this merger won't result in any job loss." If layoffs are forthcoming, the leader will not be trusted in the future. Layoffs themselves may not erode trust, but false promises do.

Leaders can gain trust through being consistent in words and deeds in a variety of ways that group members will recognize. A sampling of these behaviors follow:

- Tell employees you trust them and then follow it up with open-book management in which employees are privy to financial information about the company. Educating employees about how a company makes money, what its profits are, and other financial information is important. It reduces suspicion and ignorance about company finances, elevates trust, and improves morale.

- Avoid *mixed messages*. Leaders who deliver a consistent message are trusted the most.
- Ask for feedback on how well your intentions are lining up with your behavior. Ask riveting questions such as, "What commitments have I made that I didn't follow through?"
- Keep careful track of what you promise group members, and verify for yourself whether words and deeds correspond.
- Conduct yourself in the way you ask others to conduct themselves. If you preach that others should practice good human relations, practice good human relations yourself.
- Minimize hypocrisy. For example, if you condemn others for wasting corporate resources, don't take elaborate business trips for yourself or ornately decorate your office. During Michael Ovitz's brief stay as the president of Disney Corporation, he hired six secretaries for himself while preaching frugality. As a result, some Disney employees distrusted him.
- Tell the truth. It is much easier to be consistent when you do not have to keep patching up your story to conform to an earlier lie.

Key Word

A **mixed message** is a communication that has a built-in inconsistency or discrepancy, such as saying to the sales staff, "Complete honesty is our policy, but remember to charge whatever the traffic will bear."

Advisor

It takes a leader a long time to build trust, yet one brief incident of untrustworthy behavior can permanently destroy trust. Leaders are usually allowed a fair share of honest mistakes. In contrast, dishonest mistakes erode leadership effectiveness quickly. You may recall the military leader assigned to a commission on sexual harassment who was later charged with sexual harassment himself. The officer's credibility plummeted faster than the stock market after the Federal Reserve hikes interest rates.

Stop Wearing Your Sunglasses Indoors

Developing the trust of others generally involves your inner core and your actions. If you communicate your ethical beliefs and if your actions match your words, group members will trust you. However, it is also important to *look* trustworthy.

Certain aspects of appearance and other facets of nonverbal behavior communicate the message that a person can be trusted. Some nonverbal indicators suggest a person of questionable trustworthiness. You can consciously control whether you show some of these indicators of trust or distrust. Other indicator behaviors are based on your genes and are therefore tough to modify.

Give careful consideration to the following aspects of nonverbal behavior that influence whether others will readily perceive you to be trustworthy or untrustworthy:

- Smiling frequently suggests authenticity as opposed to smiling constantly, which suggests a cover-up for real feelings.
- Smiling symmetrically suggests authenticity. In contrast, a crooked smile suggests duplicity.
- Flashing brief smiles and other facial expressions such as frowning suggests authenticity. In contrast, prolonged facial expressions suggest a lack of authenticity.
- Maintaining eye contact without staring sends a signal of trustworthiness.
- Being well dressed sends a signal of trustworthiness. However, don't be so well dressed that it appears you are hiding behind your clothing.
- Being well coifed helps create an impression of trustworthiness. However, your hair shouldn't be so gorgeous that it commands more attention than you do.
- Maintaining a relaxed, easy manner in front of others instead of fidgeting projects trust.

Watch Out!
In addition to nonverbal indicators of trustworthiness, avoid projecting suspicion by constantly using phrases such as, "To be candid," "Let me be honest with you," "To tell the truth," and "Trust me on this one." All of these expressions send the gentle hint that on other occasions, you are not so truthful.

- Using a friendly, warm gaze instead of a beady-eyed look helps you appear trustworthy.
- Generally looking ahead and sideways contributes to a trustworthy image. Suddenly and frequently turning your head around makes others think you are paranoid and, therefore, difficult to trust.
- Keeping your eyes generally at least two-thirds open suggests trustworthiness, but squinting looks dishonest.
- Frequent nose rubbing usually suggests dishonesty or at least severe unease.
- Wearing sunglasses indoors (unless you are a celebrity, sports figure, or other entertainer) connotes deception and perhaps criminal activity.

The Least You Need to Know

- Achieve credibility by showing integrity.
- Develop your own personal code to guide your daily decision-making.
- Test the ethics of a contemplated decision by running the decision through a six-point test.
- Develop a consistency between words and deeds by "walking the talk."
- Project an image of trustworthiness by an honest appearance.

All About Goals

by Jeff Davidson

So, you have a goal or two you'd like to achieve. What will it actually take to make this goal a reality in your life? Heck, you can be setting goals from now until your dying day, but that doesn't mean you're going to reach any of them.

You're a serious type of person, though, and you don't intend to engage in idle fantasy. This time around, you aim to reach your goals.

You know what? You actually can! You have what it takes to make your goals a reality. Otherwise, you would have never had such a notion to begin with. Although people all around you are setting goals in an almost frivolous manner (making a half-baked New Year's resolution that is all but forgotten within three days), you're different. You've got some specific things you want to achieve, a quality of life you want to attain, and even certain ways you want to feel. You're not going to settle for symbolic success—you want the real McCoy. If this describes your situation to a tee, flip the page.

Introduction

As a fundamental notion of goal setting, I want you to immediately understand that whether or not you actively set goals, you are always pursuing them. It benefits you to actively set goals, because this gives you greater control of your life and career. That, of course, is what you seek. Let the couch potatoes with six-packs do what they do (unless you're married to one and can't stand it any longer!).

Meanwhile, you've got work to do. You want to better your life and have more fulfilling relationships, more enriching experiences, and more peak moments. You're not content to let *The Simpsons* or *Seinfeld* reruns be your primary form of relaxation and relief. You know there's more within your grasp.

For whatever you're seeking, recognize this: You wouldn't even harbor the notion unless there was some capacity for its attainment within you. Given that you maintain worthwhile, positive goals that do not diminish the rights of others, your quest represents a highly worthwhile pursuit for you and, potentially, many others. After all, those who have achieved substantial and outrageous goals often end up benefiting society. Nelson Mandela's personal pursuit for freedom and justice eventually led to a greater level of freedom and justice for the people of an entire nation and many other people throughout the world. The same is true of Lech Walesa in Poland and Vaclav Havel in the Czech Republic.

Michael Jordan's personal pursuit of athletic excellence in basketball simultaneously led to a ton of championships for the Chicago Bulls and provided inspiration and enjoyment for several hundred million people throughout the world. The same can be said for the personal pursuit of excellence of Placido Domingo in operatic singing, Ralph Nader in consumerism, Betty Ford in chemical-dependency recovery, Dr. David Ho in AIDS research, Mother Theresa in helping the poor, and Tom Hanks in motion pictures.

Chapter 12

What Is a Goal as Opposed to a Wish?

In This Chapter

- When you wish upon a star
- Goal setting for the new year
- Effective goal-setting techniques
- Goal setting versus useless gestures

When you wish upon a star, you're wasting your time. Stars are simply great masses of inflamed gases light years away from Earth. They are visible to the naked eye because of their sheer magnitude and luminescence. They, however, have no effect on your life, the goals you're seeking to reach, or anything else about you. If you think I'm belaboring the point, it's only because so many people engage in wishing instead of effective goal setting. It's enough to make anybody want to head for the stars and stay there.

This chapter lays the groundwork on setting and reaching your goals. After completing it, you'll be able to differentiate between goals and other things that seem like goals.

A Wish versus a Goal

"I wish I could get a big raise."

"I wish I could save some money."

"I wish I could travel around the world."

If you've had any such wishes recently or over the years, is it likely you've made any progress toward them? If you hear others make such wishes, do you suspect for a second they're actually going to attain them? Hardly.

A wish is a daydream—a fleeting fantasy about how things might be. It might be one time or recurring. It might be within or totally beyond the realms of possibility. The common denominator of all wishes is that they are not attached to a plan of action.

Wishes Have Their Place

I'm not knocking wishes, per se; they do have their place. Wishes, fantasies, and daydreams all serve a purpose, including these:

- They temporarily relieve you from a trying situation.
- They build up your anticipation for something that might occur in the future.
- They help you see new possibilities.
- They lay the groundwork for what might become a goal.

This last purpose is particularly worth examining. A wish can be the forerunner to a goal. In other words, by wishing something were so, you might take the steps to make it so. The gap for many people between wishing and taking action, however, is large. Too many people, I fear, are content to wish their lives away.

"I wish I could lose 10 pounds."

"I wish I could get the boss to notice me."

"I wish I had the time to take my kids to the circus."

Wishes Can Lose Power

One of the dangers of continually wishing without taking action toward those wishes is that your wish actually begins to lose power. Have you ever wanted something so badly or for so long, done little to achieve it, and then one day realized that you didn't really want it after all? Sure—we all have.

What happens when you continually want something but make no effort whatsoever to achieve it? In a sense, you're confusing your inner being. On the one hand, part of you is longing for what you don't have. On the other hand, another large part of you intrinsically recognizes that you're

- Making no plans
- Expending no energy
- Taking no action

That part of you concludes that you don't really want this after all. Therefore, you are in a state of perpetual frustration. You apparently want something and, concurrently, are behaviorally locked from taking action.

What Is a Goal?

"Okay," you ask, "what specifically is a goal?" So much has been written about goals over the years that I hardly know where to begin. Because you want hard-core information boiled down to its essence, I'm going to give you the most practical and simple definition of a goal.

Here it is in three words: *a desired outcome.* That says it all:

- "Desired" says it's something you're seeking, something you want, and something you're willing to strive for and lend energy to.
- "Outcome" means a result. It's a situation you can describe, an achievement to which you can point, and a feeling that is real and unmistakable.

> **Uh-Oh!**
> In your own life, if you wish upon a star, or say one thing but do something entirely different, is it likely you're going to achieve any of your goals? Not!

The Sword in the Stone

Certainly, after achieving a desirable outcome, you're not fixed in stone; you can set new goals beyond those you've achieved. It's also very important that you enjoy yourself in the pursuit of your goal.

You've heard the old expression, "Life is a journey, not a destination." So too, pursuit of your goals is as much a journey as a destination. As a classic illustration, what value would your goal have if it was to earn a million dollars, but you chewed up 30 years of your life earning that million, were miserable all that time, and now have nothing to show for it but the money—all other aspects of your life suffered?

On the other hand, people such as

- Teachers who want to empower their students,
- Spouses who want to have strong and happy marriages, and
- Ecologists who want to enjoy interacting with nature every day, all have lifetime goals that can be achieved a little each day and are enjoying the trip as much as they will the destination.

Assumptions About You!

I'm going to make some assumptions about the goals you seek to pursue before getting into more specific information about goal setting:

- Your goals are of a positive nature. They are designed to propel you forward in your life and career.
- Your goals do not interfere with the rights of others. They don't jeopardize anyone's safety or well-being.
- Your goals, however outrageous or lofty, are based on reality—for example, your goals are not to return to the year 1820, become immortal, or distort the fundamental atomic structure.
- You intend to support your goals through energy and effort.

If your goals don't fit what I've described here, stop reading!

Goal Setting for the New Year

Go for the Gold! The mere fact that you made a resolution often means that there is a larger issue behind it that is valid and worth tackling.

Legions of people commit the all too common mistake of setting goals for the new year. Such New Year's resolutions hardly ever result in the outcome the person making the resolution wanted. Why?

In her book *The Art of the Fresh Start*, Glenna Salsbury says that "Resolutions usually are designed to fix or improve a surface problem or concern or habit in life without looking at the root cause of our dissatisfaction." She believes that if people have too much stress or too many preoccupations, they will not be likely to muster the energy needed to sustain a commitment to that resolution.

If you told me that this year, you're going to take more vacations or lose 10 pounds, I'd be willing to believe that you're probably working long and hard, so the idea of vacations came to you. Perhaps you're a little overweight and the idea of losing weight is appealing.

So, as the new year rolls around, go ahead and make resolutions if it makes you feel better, but recognize that unless you put effort behind them, they'll be useless gestures.

Developing Effective Goal-Setting Techniques

Goal setting is a complex process that takes into account a person's psychological and physiological makeup. Because you bought this book with the express purpose of getting to the root of what it takes to set and reach your goals, though, I'm going to clear away all the excess and boil down goal setting to the absolute fundamentals.

You only need to be aware of three elements. So, drum roll please…

- Your goal needs to be challenging but reachable.
- Your goal has to be quantifiable.
- Your goal needs to be associated with some timeline.

In this section, you'll look at each of these elements in detail.

Challenging but Reachable

Suppose that you're 25 years old, have just graduated with a Ph.D. in political science from an Ivy League school, and are considered brilliant by everyone who knows you. Your goal is to become a U.S. senator within the next three years. You have the academic credentials, family background, connections, good appearance, strong voice, and well-developed views that foster a large constituency in contemporary society.

The only problem is that your goal is unreachable. Why? You forgot one thing about running for the U.S. Senate. You have to be at least 30 years old.

Not totally out of the question, you say? You could lobby members of Congress to bring about change. Perhaps 28 should be the minimum. After all, in many respects, people are more knowledgeable today than their counterparts of generations ago.

Even if you could start working to have this reform enacted, is it likely that it would happen in time for you to run for office and be elected by age 28? If so, it's a long shot.

Suppose that you're a woman in NASA and aspire to be the first woman to walk on the moon. NASA has no plans for having any "manned" probes of the moon scheduled for the next three decades.

So, what's an ambitious female astronaut to do? Get into the policy and planning division of NASA, redirect it toward the moon, and then find a way to be in the next ship headed there?

Boldly Going Where No One Has Gone Before

In these scenarios, the goals set by the individuals are challenging but unreachable.

As a general principle, if your goal involves achieving something that no one in history has achieved, such as redirecting large institutions or a government agency or vastly exceeding your organization's historical norms, it's reasonably safe to conclude that the goal you've chosen is unreachable. Notice that I didn't say unworthy or unmerited.

Work for Change

In the first scenario, the brilliant political science student certainly could work toward enacting change, enabling people who are 28 or perhaps 25 to run for the Senate. I think it's a wonderful idea. There are brilliant minds among us who are less than 30 years old who could do a bang-up job. When you consider the performance of some current Senators, the argument is all the more sound.

Nevertheless, a challenging but reachable goal, in this case, would be to become a senator by age 30, which, on rare occasions, *has been* achieved by a few people.

For Sure

John F. Kennedy became a senator by age 35 as his father paved and paid the way with millions of dollars, as well as business and political influence that many people can't even begin to imagine. Mr. Kennedy then became U.S. president at the tender age of 43—again with the massive aid of his father's money and influence.

Head for a Different Target

The female astronaut certainly could start pushing papers, making speeches, lobbying members of Congress, and working within NASA to redirect the agency's value in resuming moon walks.

Are other options available? Always! Perhaps our astronaut could strive to be the first person to walk on Mars, a pioneer for some element of the U.S. space station, or a person who sets a new type of record for endurance or performance in space.

Don't Get Me Wrong

I want you to understand that when you're bucking up against something as large and relatively intractable as the U.S. Constitution, the prevailing political climate, a government agency, or any other institution or organization with decades of history, it's important to understand the scope of the effort necessary to break the tide.

To tackle highly challenging goals that you deem reachable, I suggest that you do the following:

- Understand the turf. Look at the historical record, talk to insiders, and read about where things are headed.
- Prepare to commit yourself on a level you might not have considered.
- Check your time horizon. Is the goal challenging but reachable within the time limit you've given yourself?
- Identify crucial resources. Who else or what else do you need to make this goal a reality?

Pursuing Quantifiable Goals

The second major element for effective goal setting is to choose goals that are quantifiable. So often, you hear somebody say, "I want to be the top salesperson in the company." What does that mean?

> **Word Power**
> If something is *quantifiable*, that means you can measure or count it.

Let me tell you a little story. While driving a rental car in Kansas to a convention where I was speaking, I heard an advertisement on the radio. The president of some car dealership was saying that he was striving to be "the largest car dealer in the state." Seems like a lofty goal, but what could that mean?

The Largest What?

When I got to the hotel, for the fun of it, I took a piece of paper and started writing all the possibilities. Here is a *partial* list of the many meanings I derived from the unquantified goal of being the largest car dealer in the state:

- To have the most amount of cars available for sale
- To have the largest annual sales volume
- To have the largest lot or largest showroom
- To have the highest profits
- To have the most dealership branches
- To have the most sales representatives
- To have the greatest number of car models available for show
- To have the greatest number of buyers
- To be the heaviest owner (weigh the most!) among car dealerships in the state

Unleashed Ambiguity

I could go on with at least 20 other possible meanings for being the largest car dealer in the state. As you can surmise, because this goal was stated in a non-specific way (to be the largest), it lacks the specificity to provide those who have such a goal with marshaling effort, energy, and attention.

The specific goal of having the highest sales revenue among car dealerships in the state would require a different approach than the specific goal of having the most amount of vehicles available for display. Similarly, other potential meanings would require different steps for their realizations.

> **Uh-Oh!**
>
> 
>
>
> If your goal is to be the best at something in your organization, on your athletic team, or in your personal life in general, watch out! Being the best doesn't have a quantity attached to it, so it's hard to know when you've reached your goal.

A Specific Timeline

The third essential element of effective goal setting is to have a specific timeline. This involves simply attaching some date or time unit to the end of your goal statement. If your goal is to achieve a 10 percent pay increase, for example, you can add a specific timeline to your goal such as the following:

- My goal is to achieve a 10 percent pay increase by December 31st of this year.
- My goal is to achieve a 10 percent increase in pay within 12 months from now.
- My goal is to achieve a 10 percent pay increase by the end of the next quarter.
- My goal is to achieve a 10 percent increase in pay within six months after completing my degree.

All these statements represent valid timelines associated with a specific quantifiable goal—achieving a 10 percent pay increase.

Why Goal Setting Is Misunderstood

So much has been written and said about goals, it's easy to understand why goal setting often is misunderstood. This section looks at some common myths about goal setting and the realities.

Goals Set for You by Others Won't Work

There's a common misperception that a goal you undertake has to be your own, devised by you, set by you, and pursued by you. This is not true. Studies have shown that it's entirely possible for one person to set goals for another and to have the entire process work. In fact, this happens every day in sales organizations where sales managers develop quotas for the sales staff.

The key element here is to have the person for whom the goal is set adopt the goals as his or her own. The fact that goals set by others can be met is welcome news for parents, managers, or anyone who has the inherent or mandated responsibility for the performance of others.

Never Tamper with a Set Goal

This is true much of the time, but there are enough exceptions to merit discussion. Often, when you set an appropriate goal, factors outside your control change. Some of these changes could include

- A new regulation levied by government.
- Something a competitor has done.
- A change in the social environment.
- A significant reduction or increase in resources allocated to you.

Any one of a number of factors can change in your environment, so there are times when it makes sense to revise your goals midstream. Now, I'm not saying that this is an open-ended excuse to modify goals on a whim or when the going gets tough. Instead, it's a simple recognition that even the most intelligently and appropriately set goals sometimes cannot withstand the fluctuations of a changing environment.

> **Go for the Gold!**
> Set challenging and reachable goals that are quantifiable and have a specific timeline. Pursue them with vigor. All the while, recognize that they might end up as stepping stones to other goals that emerge as you realize one desirable outcome after another.

A Goal Is an End in Itself

Although a goal *can* be an end in itself, it rarely is. If your goal is to achieve an increase in earnings, a reduction in weight, or a better-quality relationship, ask yourself what's behind that.

In the case of increased earnings, it might be to better afford the education of your children, enjoy greater leisure, or donate more to worthy causes. In the case of reducing weight, the ends might involve having a healthier lifestyle, reducing your risk of heart attack, and increasing your longevity so that you'll be around to enjoy your grandchildren. Even having a better relationship might not be an end in itself. Other goals beyond that might be to create such abundance as a couple that the overflow enriches others, to be better role models for your children, or to spur each other to even greater growth and personal development.

It's also vital to recognize that many people are not content with the goals they set and achieve for themselves. That's why people who initially had the goal of graduating from college sometimes find themselves seeking master's degrees and then doctorates.

I know many multimillionaires, and not one of them is content with his or her current net worth. Even in my own career, after establishing myself as a speaker and author on business and career-related topics, I had a hankering for delving more deeply into self-help and personal-development topics. That's why I wrote books on managing time, reducing stress, being more assertive, and setting goals. Not surprisingly, as a professional speaker, my topics also shifted to those areas.

You Have to Go Public with Your Goal

Many goal-setting gurus advocate making your goal public. This could involve sharing your goal with others who act as reinforcers to help you achieve what you set out to do by publishing your goal in a department newsletter or broadcasting it at a meeting.

I think such measures can be useful and effective, depending on who you are, what your goal is, and how you can best pursue it. It's not essential, however, for all your goals to always be publicized.

> CAUTION!
>
> **Uh-Oh!**
> Announcing your goals can have disastrous effects in some situations. Why? You might be locked into having to achieve your goal at a visible and measurable pace so that *others* feel comfortable about your progress.

Even Progress Is Best

Sometimes the pace isn't even in the pursuit of your goal, even though you take a balanced, incremental approach. Weight loss particularly does not follow such a pattern.

Research has shown that in the first few weeks, your weight is not likely to change at all. Your body is adjusting to new levels of exercise and caloric intake, as well as a new rate of metabolism. Often, the greatest change comes after you might have expected it. This explains why so many people give up on diets too soon. Just when they are about to see progress toward their goal, they conclude that it's not working.

Chip Away at Your Goal a Little at a Time

I mentioned in the introduction that incremental progress toward pursuing goals will work as well as anything. That's true, but it's also true that sometimes your perceived progress is anything but incremental. This uneven progression is called *germination*.

> **Word Power**
> *Germination,* which in biology means sprouting, can mean development, growth, or maturation; none of these concepts suggests an even progression.

When learning to play the piano, for example, you might have the darndest time practicing a particular song. Suppose that you try something a bit more complicated. After spending days attempting to learn the more complicated piece, you return to the easier piece.

Guess what? All of a sudden, you can play it with a flourish. Why? You experienced germination while learning to play the piano. As you jumped to the more difficult piece, you were laying the foundation for being able to effectively play the easier piece *even though you weren't practicing it.* This seemingly uneven type of progression happens all the time.

> **For Sure**
> In his book *Maximum Success,* Brian Tracy says that your pursuit of success is rarely an even progression. It's more like two steps forward and one step back.

Goal Setting versus Useless Gestures

Okay, you've learned that it's best to approach your goals while maintaining balance and proceeding with relative simplicity. You know that an incremental approach to reaching your goals will work as well as anything, although attainment of your goals rarely follows a smooth progression. You also know that you want to set challenging, reachable goals that are quantifiable and have specific timelines.

What's the difference, then, between goal setting and useless gestures?

Merely Discussing or Contemplating Your Goal

If you only talk about your goal, it's a nearly useless gesture. It is possible to mentally maintain a goal without writing it down, but the probabilities are on the side of writing it down.

> **Go for the Gold!**
> By recording your goals on paper or on your computer, you have an increased probability of attaining them, if for no other reason than that you have the opportunity to review what you've written or typed. What's more, the act of logging your goals is a reinforcing process.

It's kind of analogous to listening to a brilliant lecture and taking brilliant notes. The notes are your own, in your own hand, and have particular relevance for you. Suppose that the lecturer distributed notes for you, though, and you didn't need to take notes at all. You'd probably be less inclined to apply or act on things contained in the prepared handout than on the page of notes you personally recorded.

I suppose that the best of all worlds is when you get a prepared handout and make notes on top of that. In any case, the fact that you recorded with your own hands information, insights, or suggestions for action increases the probability that you actually will do something with what you've written.

Goals you've set when you're light-headed, tipsy, or outright inebriated aren't worth the barroom napkin they're scribbled on—unless, of course, you later examine it, determine its relevance, and make the effort to pursue those goals.

Setting goals as a boast or challenge also is often a useless gesture. Although competition can induce participants to turn in stronger performances, boasting often produces the wrong kind of energy, particularly if you're talking about goal attainment that requires long-term efforts.

For Sure

If one shot-putter in the Olympics lets fly an Olympic record heave, statistics show that the other participants in the contest often exceed their average as well because they are stirred by the competition. Sprinters in the 100-meter dash come within hundredths of a second of each other and often exceed their personal bests because of intense competition.

Boasting, particularly in the face of your competition, can backfire. If you tell an opposing team "We're going to whip your butts," they're likely to play harder to show you how wrong you are. You might notice that when athletes refer to other teams they're about the face, they often say something respectful. This is an intelligent and psychological ploy to avoid giving the other team something they can be riled by or use for inspiration.

For Sure

The most notable exception to the strategy of not riling the opposition in the annals of sports is Mohammed Ali.

Ali would boast to reporters, onlookers, and his boxing opponent that he would win by a knockout in a certain round. He used rhyming phrases like, "You'll barely be alive at the end of five," or "The world will end before you last 10" as a way to psychologically intimidate his opponent. In Ali's case, using boasts to announce his goal worked. In your case, I'm suggesting that you play it a little safer and not boast.

Not Revisiting Your Goal

Perhaps the all-time useless gesture is to make a goal—even writing it down or saving it to a disk—and then not revisit it often enough for it to be effective. This is somewhat similar to what most people do when making a New Year's resolution. You identify a desirable outcome, but then you remind yourself of your quest to achieve this outcome so infrequently that it loses potency.

The Least You Need to Know

- When you wish upon a star, you're wasting your time.
- In the simplest terms, a *goal* is a desirable outcome.
- In the best of all worlds, you achieve your goals with balance and relative simplicity, a little bit at a time.
- Effective goal setting involves selecting challenging, reachable, and quantifiable goals that are associated with a timeline.
- It's entirely possible to achieve the goals set for you by others if you internalize the goals and make them your own.

Chapter 13

The Seven Basic Goal Categories

In This Chapter

- Seven categories of human needs
- Staying positive
- Brainstorm your way to novel ideas
- The Thought-Diet Card

Too often, when you pick up a book or article on setting and reaching your goals, you encounter a variety of terms; some of these terms are helpful, but many can cloud the issue. What's the difference between an objective and a goal, a goal and a strategy, a priority and a strategy, a tactic and a maneuver, a mission and a mission statement, and so on? There are good books that define these terms in ways that make sense, but I'm going to cut through the clutter and keep the terminology as simple as possible. I simply define a *goal* as something you want to reach or a desired outcome.

While pursuing your goals, you might rely on action steps, strategies, tactics, maneuvers, or other procedures. The terms you use are largely irrelevant. You set a goal, you do things to reach that goal, and you reach the goal. Then, you set another. Does this sound good to you?

The Key Areas of Life

In looking for a goal-setting model, I turned to an expert on the topic—a champion goal setter and goal reacher in his own right, Dr. Tony Alessandra. Dr. Alessandra has written 12 books, including *The Platinum Rule* and *Charisma*, both published by Warner Books. He also has created dozens of award-winning video and cassette programs.

His popular Web site, **http://www.platinumrule.com**, receives up to 4,000 visitors a month. At the site, Dr. Alessandra offers a self-scoring quiz you can take to quickly and easily determine which of four basic personality types you fit into and how you can best interrelate with others. You can even take the quiz for a friend or spouse. In other words, you answer the questions based on what you know about that person, and you get information back telling you how to best relate with him or her.

Dr. Alessandra's basic strategy (on which the rest of this chapter is based) is simple yet profound. He contends that your life is a system. You can't view what you do at work as separate from what you do at home, and vice versa.

In this chapter, I discuss the seven goal areas Dr. Alessandra cites as common to most people—key elements of life, including mental, physical, family, social, career, spiritual, and financial goals.

The Big Seven

Dr. Alessandra says that for many years, people lived with the mistaken belief that their home life and work life could be totally separate. Many people gave their families and personal lives a back seat to their careers, chasing only the carrot of success while other facets of their lives suffered. Yet, you have many needs and wants you seek to fulfill. Basically, human needs fall into seven broad categories:

- Mental: The functions of your mind—memory, concentration, learning, creativity, reasoning, and mathematical abilities
- Physical: The many functions of your body—overall fitness, percent of body fat, skills and abilities, agility, and endurance
- Family: Your relationships with the special people you consider to be part of your family
- Social: Your relationships with others outside your family and outside your business—in a word, *friends*

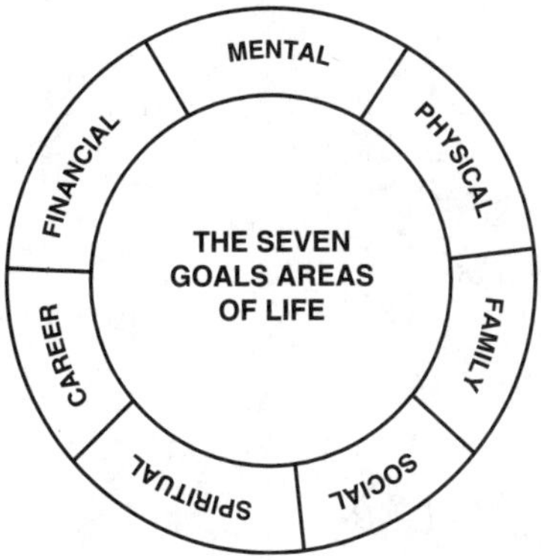

- Spiritual: Your relationship between you and your Creator—also defined as the philosophical and humanitarian areas of your life
- Career: Your involvement in your chosen field, both on and off the job
- Financial: The management of your financial resources and obligations

Oh, So Delicate a Balance

In many ways, you are like a fragile ecosystem. The elements of your life are interdependent. One need affects the others, especially when it is grossly neglected.

> **Go for the Gold!**
> Creating balance among the seven need categories in your life is particularly important. Each category can positively or negatively affect the others, depending on the attention or lack of attention it receives.

Everyone knows that financial problems affect your outlook, health, social life, and family life, for example. That's why practitioners of holistic medicine examine all facets of a person's life when they search for the cause of a physical illness.

You are a complex being with complex needs. Moreover, your needs are dynamic rather than static—they are always changing. At one point in your life, your career pursuits may require more time than your spiritual or family needs. At some other time, another need may be emphasized more than the others.

Goals as Targets

Striving for and attaining a balance of goals makes life meaningful. Yet, for all that has ever been written about goals, the great masses of people haven't much to show for it.

> *Most people aim at nothing in life…and hit it with amazing accuracy.*
> —Anonymous

Such a statement is a sad commentary about people, but it is true. Lewis Carroll eloquently stated this point in *Alice's Adventures in Wonderland*:

> **Uh-Oh!**
> Having one need that is more urgent than others doesn't mean that the others disappear. They, too, must receive at least a minimal amount of your attention. You rarely can neglect a need completely without suffering unpleasant consequences.

Alice: Mr. Cat, which of these paths shall I take?

Cheshire Cat: Well, my dear, where do you want to go?

Alice: I don't suppose it really matters.

Cheshire Cat: Then, my dear, any path will do!

If you have no goals, or more likely, vague or hazy notions about goals, don't be surprised if you find yourself feeling emotionally, socially, spiritually, physically, or professionally unbalanced. It's a sign of strength when you make decisions that positively affect the direction of your life.

Stumbling into Great Achievement

Does anyone ever stumble into great achievement? Even when a lab researcher discovers something extraordinary by accident, the discovery usually follows years of hard work.

Can you imagine the following exchange taking place after Sir Edmund Hillary returned from Mount Everest?

> Reporter: Congratulations, Sir Hillary! Tell me, why did you become the first man to conquer Mount Everest?
>
> Sir Hillary: I was wandering around trying to become inspired when I ended up on the top of this mountain.

Reporter: Really! Did it work?

Sir Hillary: Yes, but by the time I got back, I forgot why I went up to begin with.

Of course, this scenario is absurd, because such a monumental feat as climbing Mount Everest requires serious goal setting and attainment. Sir Hillary had to work hard to gain the knowledge and physical skills necessary for the climb. He also had to acquire the help of a team of experts and procure all the equipment. His preparation took an enormous amount of time—longer than the climb itself.

A Road Map as Good as Any

When you earnestly pursue your goals, reasons to do some things and to avoid others appear in your life. A young man from a tough neighborhood has never been involved with drugs or in trouble with the law. Do you marvel at his good fortune and strength of character?

When he was 10 years old, he set the goal of becoming an astronaut. At last report, he had graduated from the U.S. Air Force Academy with a degree in astronautical engineering. He is so focused on his goal that he avoids doing anything to hurt his chances of success.

An Easy Mark

It is easy to spot a person who has a clear set of goals. That person exudes a sense of purpose and determination. He or she has abundant energy and is willing to put more time and effort into any given task.

> **Go for the Gold!**
> Being goal oriented can even help you to become more positive, optimistic, and assertive.

People who continually set, pursue, and monitor their career goals are more productive than people who simply work at a job. The uninspired worker goes home at the end of the day having gained nothing more than a few dollars and a lot of aggravation.

When you clearly set goals in all major areas of your life, the right roads appear in front of you like mirages in the desert. Of course, unlike mirages, these roads are real! Choices become infinitely easier to make, and you'll realize that you have taken a giant step toward living a balanced life.

> **Go for the Gold!**
> People who have a clear set of goals in life exude a sense of purpose and determination, are taken seriously by others, and are respected by their peers. In contrast, those who have no goals feel emotionally, socially, spiritually, physically, and professionally unbalanced, which only causes further anxiety.

The Right Outlook

In the past two decades, much criticism has been levied at positive thinking—probably because it has been exploited and overcommercialized. However, if you are serious about succeeding in your chosen field, you'll need to cultivate positive thinking as an everyday habit.

Negative assumptions, which set up internal obstacles that can defeat you, usually become *self-fulfilling prophecies*. You assume that you cannot do something, so you then act in ways that guarantee your failure; this, in turn, reinforces your original assumption. Therefore, you must replace your negative assumptions with positive assumptions or positive thinking, which generates positive results.

Self-confidence goes hand-in-hand with positive thinking. It is the food that feeds your personal growth. It is an absolutely indispensable part of achievement. Self-confidence works best when based on your own knowledge and self-respect instead of comparisons between yourself and others. Don't compare yourself to other people, because you're likely to feel pompous or bitter, and neither of these feelings is desirable. So, your self-confidence needs to exist in a vacuum, which it can.

> **Uh-Oh!**
> Many people have an inaccurate self-concept and are negative thinkers by habit. This limited self-concept acts as a filter to limit the amount of new things they feel they are capable of doing.

A Skewed Self-Concept

Even when you are armed with positive thinking and self-confidence, something called a *self-concept* may yet be a stumbling block for you. Your self-concept is the image you have of yourself. It is the evaluation you justly or unjustly make based on everything you know (or think you know) about yourself.

When a new thought or feeling comes into your awareness, if it is consistent with your self-concept, you accept the new idea as valid. If the idea is not consistent with your self-concept, however, you tend to reject it.

Maintaining a positive self-concept is one of the most valuable things you can do for yourself, especially when it comes to considering and establishing new types of goals that may be somewhat outside the bounds of what you've considered or attempted in the past.

Getting Started Through Brainstorming

Consider the concept of *brainstorming*. This a mental technique that offers a valuable way of exploring potential goals to select in any of the seven goal categories or supporting goals you establish.

> **Go for the Gold!**
> Brainstorming is a valuable way of exploring your goals. When ideas flow freely, many more ideas, as well as more novel ideas, are generated.

Don't Judge Your Ideas

With brainstorming, you give free flight to your ideas. Let ideas flow without judging them, and you will generate many times the ideas produced through the normal reasoning process. After you generate these ideas, you can begin to evaluate their usefulness.

Here are some guidelines for brainstorming:

- *Suspend all judgment.* This is a time to remove your internal censor. Nothing is unimportant, too silly, or too wild to include when brainstorming.
- *Think quantity, not quality.* The more ideas you generate, the better your chances are of hitting on something new and useful.
- *Extrapolate and experiment.* No matter how nonsensical it might seem, take your ideas to the highest level. Combine ideas in unusual ways to stimulate new ideas.
- *Evaluate later.* Do not close your mind to any suggestions. An idea that seemed ridiculous yesterday might be ingenious tomorrow.

Brainstorming Mechanics

To brainstorm, find a time when you will not be distracted. Sit comfortably with a pencil and paper or a pocket dictator. Then form a question of a problem to be handled. Make your question specific, such as "How can I increase my level of fitness and achieve my target weight?" After you ask the question, immediately begin jotting down or recording your ideas.

> **Uh-Oh!**
> Record the first thing that comes to your mind. Do not judge your responses, or you'll short-change the process. You can fill in the details of your notes later.

If you're writing, make notes in brief phrases to save time. If you're dictating (my preferred method), use full sentences, but then quickly go back to your brainstorming mode so that other ideas may follow.

When you finish, review your notes. Examine all the possibilities. Discard unusable ideas only at the end. Continue to suspend all judgment during this exercise. Often, wild and crazy ideas, when put together or altered slightly, turn out to be your most novel, effective solutions. So let yourself go.

You might feel a little silly writing down some of the ideas. That's normal.

Applied to Your Goals

When considering your life's goals, brainstorm each category using these brainstorming guidelines. Allow about two minutes per category, using one page per category—seven pages in all. Again, shoot for quantity and let your imagination take over!

When you finish, review what you've written (or dictated) and add anything you might have forgotten or that now seems appropriate.

And the Three Winners Are...

> **Go for the Gold!**
> Circling one idea per page enables you to see your goals in black and white, on paper, where they show up best.

When you're satisfied with your responses, look them over and circle the one idea under each category that stands out as being the most important. Don't worry about what others might think of your choice.

Whether there is repetition among your seven circled "semi-finalists" from the seven groups is unimportant. Now, drum roll, please.... Examine the seven goals, and disregarding which group they came from, choose the three that are the most pressing to you.

Write those three goals on a separate sheet of paper with the title "My Three Most Important Goals." These represent the most important goals in your life at this time and undoubtedly merit time and attention. But hold on! A balanced approach to life works best.

And the Important Runners-Up Include...

As valuable as it is to isolate your most precious goals, it is equally important to remain *cognizant* of your other goals.

Review your sheet for each of your seven categories and list all the secondary goals that are worthy of action. You now have a good indication of where you are in life and where you would like to be in every facet.

As an example, here is a list that one sales representative compiled:

- Mental goals: Stop worrying so much about money and success, improve my memory of names, increase my vocabulary proficiency, broaden my knowledge
- Physical goals: Eat less junk food, do stress-reduction exercises every night, floss teeth every night, maintain an ideal weight
- Family goals: Call Mom and Dad once a week, spend at least 10 minutes daily listening to my spouse and each child
- Social goals: Go to weekly Rotary Club meetings, socialize with more salespeople, and exchange ideas
- Spiritual goals: Go to church once every two weeks, be more helpful to people every day
- Career goals: Make three more sales per week, earn a master's degree in marketing
- Financial goals: Own my own home, purchase a sports car, provide for an ample retirement fund by the time I'm 55 years old

A Framework for Reaching Your Goals

You've already looked at the importance of internalizing or personalizing your goals (especially when the goal originates from some external source). Your goal needs to be something you *want* to do rather than something you *have* to do. Even if a sales quota is imposed on you, there are many valid reasons why you may personally want to achieve that goal—among them, pride, competitive spirit, a desire to increase your income, and a quest to improve your job status.

Your Goal Needs to Be Positive

When you hang onto a thought such as *I will not smoke today*, you end up thinking more about smoking! Instead, if you think *I will maintain clear, clean lungs today*, your aim is more direct and you're bound to be more effective in your pursuit.

Write It Down, Jack

Written goals take a jump in status from being nebulous thoughts to bonafide entities on paper or on your computer! This gives you a visual reminder and confirmation of the importance of your goals. Your goals gain credibility simply from being written.

> **Go for the Gold!**
> In the movie *The Ten Commandments*, there is an oft-repeated phrase: "So let it be written, so let it be done." People are trained from childhood to give credibility to written statements. Putting it in writing gives your words more importance.

Ready for Prime Time

How will you actually apply the goals you've set for yourself? For your three primary goals and each of your secondary goals, I suggest that you do the following:

1. Determine whether each goal is challenging yet still reachable, quantifiable, and contains specific timelines—both personal and positive. If so, continue. If not, rewrite or reword your goal as clearly as possible so that it meets this criteria.
2. Examine obstacles that stand in your way. Do you maintain any negative assumptions or self-defeating thoughts? An obstacle blocks you only if you let it. Write down your innovative ways of overcoming obstacles.
3. Ask yourself why you want to achieve the goal. What kind of payoff is motivating you? It's useful and enlightening to know. Perhaps your underlying reason is not so noble or grandiose—that's okay, as long as you're clear on why you want to proceed.
4. List the steps you will take to achieve your goal. The smaller the increments, the easier they will be to accomplish.

When recording these ideas and observations on your worksheet, fill up the page completely if it helps, and keep it visible! Put your goals in a place you will see them every day. Check off items as you complete them. Use your worksheet to chart your progress, and take pride in your accomplishments.

Uh-Oh!
He who begins too much accomplishes little.
—German proverb

GOALS WORKSHEET

PRIMARY GOAL #1

BUY NEW HOME WITHIN 24 MONTHS

POTENTIAL STEPS:

- BEGIN SAVINGS PLAN
- ASK PARENTS ABOUT ONE-TIME GIFT
- INVEST MORTGAGE OPTIONS
- BEGIN VISITING SITES
- PREPARE FINANCIAL STATEMENTS
- CHECK CREDIT REPORT
- ATTEND HOME-BUYING SEMINAR

The Thought-Diet Card

Here's a goal-achieving aid that might be right for you. The *thought diet* is a tool you can use daily to become the person who will achieve your goals. It helps you stay focused on daily action in support of your goals—actions that are bite-sized and easy to accomplish.

Thought–Diet Card

Front Side:	Back Side:
My Current Primary Goal: ____________ ____________ ____________	**Minimum Daily Behaviors in each of seven areas to take me to my goal:**
Five Traits I'm developing related to the goal:	Mental____________ Physical____________
1.	Social____________
2.	Family____________
3.	Spiritual____________
4.	Career____________
5.	Financial____________

Section by Section

In the first section of the Thought-Diet Card, write your primary goal. Write out as explicitly as possible the goal that most strongly affects your motivation right now.

In the second section of the card, write the characteristics you're developing, including five key characteristics you need to develop to achieve your goal.

In the third section of the card, write the minimum daily standards you will meet every day to move closer to your goal. Again, be specific. Here are some examples of minimum daily standards:

- Mental: I will spend 15 minutes every evening doing visualization exercises.
- Physical: I will do a minimum of 5 push-ups and 10 sit-ups every morning.
- Family: I will relax over dinner and enjoy a meaningful conversation with my family.
- Social: I will take time to call one of my new friends.

- Spiritual: Each day I will do one good deed to help someone less fortunate than I.
- Career: I will read something related to my career for at least 15 minutes every day.
- Financial: I will keep a complete record of every expense.

'Til Habits Take Hold

Read the Thought-Diet Card twice daily until everything on it becomes a habit. After you develop constructive habits, you can move on to new behaviors. Then, fill out a new card and practice the new challenges every day until they become habits.

> **Go for the Gold!**
> *The secret of success is constancy of purpose.*
> —Benjamin Disraeli

You will surely (and rather painlessly!) move closer and closer to your goals.

By leading you a little at a time, the thought diet will keep you from being overwhelmed by your more lofty goals.

Optimum Mileage

Here are some suggestions for getting optimal mileage out of the thought diet:

- Read the Thought-Diet Card twice daily—in the morning when you rise and in the evening before you retire. Repetition is an integral part of learning and will help you stay on target.
- Avoid associating with people who drag you down emotionally. Associate with people who are positive and who can increase your optimism.
- Sincerely read and complete the card. Do not go through the motions! You will be kidding no one but yourself.

The Least You Need to Know

- You don't need to complicate the pursuit of your goals with all kinds of terminology; there are goals, subgoals, and steps or actions to reach them.
- Don't believe that your home life and your work life are totally separate. If you give your family and personal lives a back seat to your career, other facets of your life will suffer.
- You have many needs and wants to fulfill, in basically seven broad categories: mental, physical, family, social, spiritual, professional, and financial.
- People with a clear set of goals exude a sense of purpose and determination, positive thinking, and abundant energy.
- Brainstorming can lead you to fresh ideas about what you want and how to accomplish it. The Thought-Diet Card can make it easier to reach your goals.

Notes

Notes

Notes

Notes